Copyright © 2021 by Kirrily Lowe

All rights reserved. This book or any portion thereof may not be reproduced or used in any manner whatsoever without the express written permission of the publisher except for the use of brief quotations in a book review.

The Invisible Tree Publishing

Macquarie St, Sydney, NSW 2000

For all enquiries regarding this publication and The Invisible She Project please visit www.kirrilylowe.com.

All Scripture quotations, unless otherwise indicated, are taken from the Holy Bible, New International Version®, NIV®. Copyright ©1973, 1978, 1984, 2011 by Biblica, Inc.™ Used by permission of Zondervan. All rights reserved worldwide. www.zondervan.comThe "NIV" and "New International Version" are trademarks registered in the United States Patent and Trademark Office by Biblica, Inc.™

Scripture quotations marked TPT are from The Passion Translation®. Copyright © 2017, 2018 by Passion & Fire Ministries, Inc. Used by permission. All rights reserved. ThePassionTranslation.com.

Scripture quotations marked MSG are taken from THE MESSAGE, copyright © 1993, 2002, 2018 by Eugene H. Peterson. Used by permission of NavPress, represented by Tyndale House Publishers. All rights reserved.

Scripture quotations marked AMP are taken from the Amplified Bible, Copyright © 2015 by The Lockman Foundation. Used by permission.

Printed in Australia

First Printing, 2021

ISBN 978-0-9808447-8-8

Internal Graphic Design: Taylor-Kate Brosnahan
Book Cover Design: Taylor-Kate Brosnahan & Clint Hutchinson

THE INVISIBLE SHE

Kirrily Lowe

'Awake, awake!
Put on your strength, O Zion;
Put on your beautiful garments'

ISAIAH 52:1 NKJV

ENDORSEMENTS

Many women of all ages and backgrounds are in an identity crisis. In the media, movies and online, we have been bombarded with images of what a woman should look like in the 21st Century. Kirrily's book engages us in a biblical view. Scripture is timeless and presents us with the possibility that we are created in God's image, therefore 'all glorious within'! This message creates for us as women, the freedom from stereotypes and paints a fresh palette of who we really are in Christ. How liberating! I highly recommend this book to all women desiring to throw off the old and be clothed in the new.

Chris Pringle
Senior Pastor and Co-Founder of C3 Church SYD
and C3 Church Global

Kirrily Lowe has brought us a wonderful book filled with revelation and insight. "The Invisible She" will inspire and empower you to walk in your God-given identity, confident in the knowledge that you are loved and highly treasured. This book will challenge and provoke you to take hold of the destiny God has planned for you. I pray you enjoy this as much as I have.

Katherine Ruonala
Senior Leader, Glory City Church Brisbane
Leader of The Australian Prophetic Council

The Invisible She, written by my beautiful wife Kirrily Lowe, is a masterpiece for every woman. It is a creative road map of revelation and transformation, revealing our new identity that comes from a life hidden in Christ. This book will take you on a journey of discovery and freedom that leads us into the spacious open places of Christ's relentless redemptive love. Kirrily's refreshing insight will clothe you in your new identity and unlock and release passion and calling on the inside of you. I greatly admire Kirrily's perseverance to complete this project. It's more than a message; it is a life story of growth and transformation. Let God clothe you in colour, strength, joy, peace and dignity as you turn these pages.

Tim Lowe
Senior Minister, God In The City Church, Darlinghurst, Sydney

In this exquisite display of creativity, Kirrily Lowe takes us on a walk through the Garden, only this time- without the need to hide or cover up. The display of God's salvation is revealed to us in a wardrobe of Christ's glorious redemption of our naked state without Him, to our lives surrendered to a King who only clothes His children in royalty. I trust you cherish the love story woven for you in these pages – because this book is not only an invitation to wholeness, but an experience as we follow the threads of revelation that Kirrily collected over years of being at the feet of Jesus.

Isi de Gersigny
Leader of The NSW Prophetic Council
Senior Pastor, Jubilee Church, Sydney, Australia

I thought I had a handle on Kirrily Lowe's "Invisible She" revelation. After all, I've heard her preach it, seen her dramatise it, and watched her live it. Now she's written it and I realise I didn't have a handle on it all! The Invisible She is a beautiful and transformative read. Kirrily has made some powerful, heavenly ideas very accessible, earthing them in such a way that they can be lived out in our real lives, not just admired on a page. Read it and get ready for it's message to continue to work in your soul long after you've finished.

Vicki Simpson
International speaker
Founder "She's The Voice"

Kirrily carries a powerful message that brings timeless biblical truth in a way that is very relevant for women today. It is vital for women to know their true identity and live clothed in the garments of the Gospel. Kirrily is gifted in bringing words of truth with grace and creativity. We have no doubt this book will bring freedom to many! We were blessed to have her minister this message in our church C3 Darwin and our congregation were impacted by the revelation brought with authenticity, life and conviction.

Lars & Megan Halvorsen
Senior Pastors, C3 Church Darwin
Leaders of C3 Australia

With deep insight and creative genius the gorgeous and gifted Kingdom Abassadress, Kirrily Lowe has translated priceless Spirit truth into musings of narrative and poetic brilliance, along with a collaboration of stunning designs. I absolutely love the uniqueness of this book and sense The Invisible She will capture imaginations and hearts around the globe to become the spiritual woman's Look Book for every season.

Elly Webb
Senior Pastor, C3 Spectrum Church, Port Stephens, Australia

Kirrily Lowe is a creative genius with a keen eye for fashion and a gift of poetry. She exposes the "clothing" of this world and the enemy's tactics to strangle our future. She then reveals the "clothing" that Jesus Christ would want each of us to dress in. She shows us that the world wants to sell you an image, but God wants to give you and I an identity. This book explains to each one of us how to be released from the bondage of performance to the freedom of calling. Read it and allow God to reclothe you – you'll never be the same.

Sue Botta
Senior Minister, C3 Church Carlingford
Overseer C3 South Asia

We are thrilled for our dear friend, Kirrily, to see this book birthed and available for women. Over the years, in different formats, we've had the privilege of hearing snippets from the pages you're about to read. Throughout this book, Kirrily weaves in her prophetic vision and expresses it in a beautiful combination of creative poetry and sound doctrine. Kirrily draws parallels from beauty in natural garments to beauty in Christ's garments, which we're called to be clothed in. If you read this book like a mirror, it will unmask the struggles commonly faced by women, and lead you on a discovery
to your true worth and identity. It will heal your past, allow your present to be reconciled, and release you into your future.

Carolyn and Claude Carrello
Senior Pastors, Awaken City Church, Rockingham, Western Australia

I believe Kirrily Lowe has written a book in which every woman can find herself. So often as I read it, I thought - yes that is me - I have experienced this too. Kirrily has a unique insight into the pain and wounds of the heart of women, and describes these conditions with honesty, compassion and creativity, which allows the reader to be vulnerable and open. However, the best things about Kirrily as an author is that she doesn't leave you in your pain, she constantly points to the One who is the answer to the pain - Jesus! This book is about the great exchange – our rags for His robe – and Kirrily explores all aspects of this exchange. This is not a theology book – but it will lead you into the truth of who Jesus is and what this can mean for your life. If you go on the journey this book invites you into – it will cause you to be clothed in Christ in a fresh and impacting new way.

Pam Borrow
Principal C3 College, Sydney, Australia

'The Invisible She' is a work of literary art. It weaves poetry, design and fashion with divine truth to create a breathtaking fabric that represents God's heart toward His daughters. Kirrily is a talented writer and poet, an accomplished leader and a committed pastor with a gift for drawing out God's purpose in the women she ministers to. 'The Invisible She' harnesses all of these qualities to connect with the heart of every woman and unveil God's vision for their life.

Janine Kubala
Senior Pastor, C3 Believe, Wollongong, Australia
Director, Kubala Ministries
Founder, Esther's Voice

Kirrily's latest book "Invisible She" is her heart on a page. This releasing and powerful message of the fierce feminine soul is not just a good idea, but her life's work. Kirrily's passion for freedom, empowerment and a life lived strong, release the reader to not only dream again but to remember where their strength comes from. I couldn't put it down. The poetry, the imagined possibilities and the imagery will help you to remember not only who you are but whose you are also. I cannot wait to hear the stories across the planet of people who have been changed by the beauty of this book.

Amanda Viviers
Author, Speaker and Radio Presenter

The Invisible She, is a poetic piece of workmanship steeped in scripture, divine imagery and overflowing with grace. My heart and soul were profoundly touched as I journeyed through each chapter, walking through His heavenly wardrobe. Kirrily has beautifully woven the heavenly with the practical, through her own life stories and biblical insight. The Invisible She moves the reader at the deepest level where faith is born. You cannot read this book and not be changed.

Heidi Wysman
Minister, Writer and Radio Presenter of 'Godspots' at Hope 103.2

My friend Kirrily lives out the God-breathed words in this book. She lives in pursuit of this King and the Invisible She message is etched into the fibre of her being, her life, her responses to life, and to the world entrusted for her to steward. This has been costly to write. It's cost her everything. And in yielding, she has been enlarged. Her life, leadership and love bears witness to the fact. Now the world gets to know you Kirrily and your life message. Thank you. Deep, deep love and respect for you. Across the oceans I am so grateful for the day our souls collided.

Vanessa Hoyes
Senior Pastor, Resurgent Church, Montreal, Canada
Life and Leadership Coach

'The Invisible She' is a poetic incarnation of the gospel. Kirrily's rawness is an invitation to find purpose in your pain. As your heart is laid bare, you will find yourself clothed by Love Himself. The absence of pretence in this book is a glimpse into Kirrily's heart; refreshing, healing and a creative overflow of God's eternal Truth. The world needs to experience this book.

Rachel Waters
Senior Minister, Selah Church, Mumbai, India

PROLOGUE

There is a woman you are created to be,
A woman Christ can already see,
And as together, He opens our eyes,
And bravely we remove our disguise,
The colour and wonder of all things good,
The natural fit for womanhood,
Dresses our Invisible She,
With a wardrobe designed for the free.
So, come now, bathe in word and truth,
And let this wardrobe renew your youth.

With love,

Kirrily xx

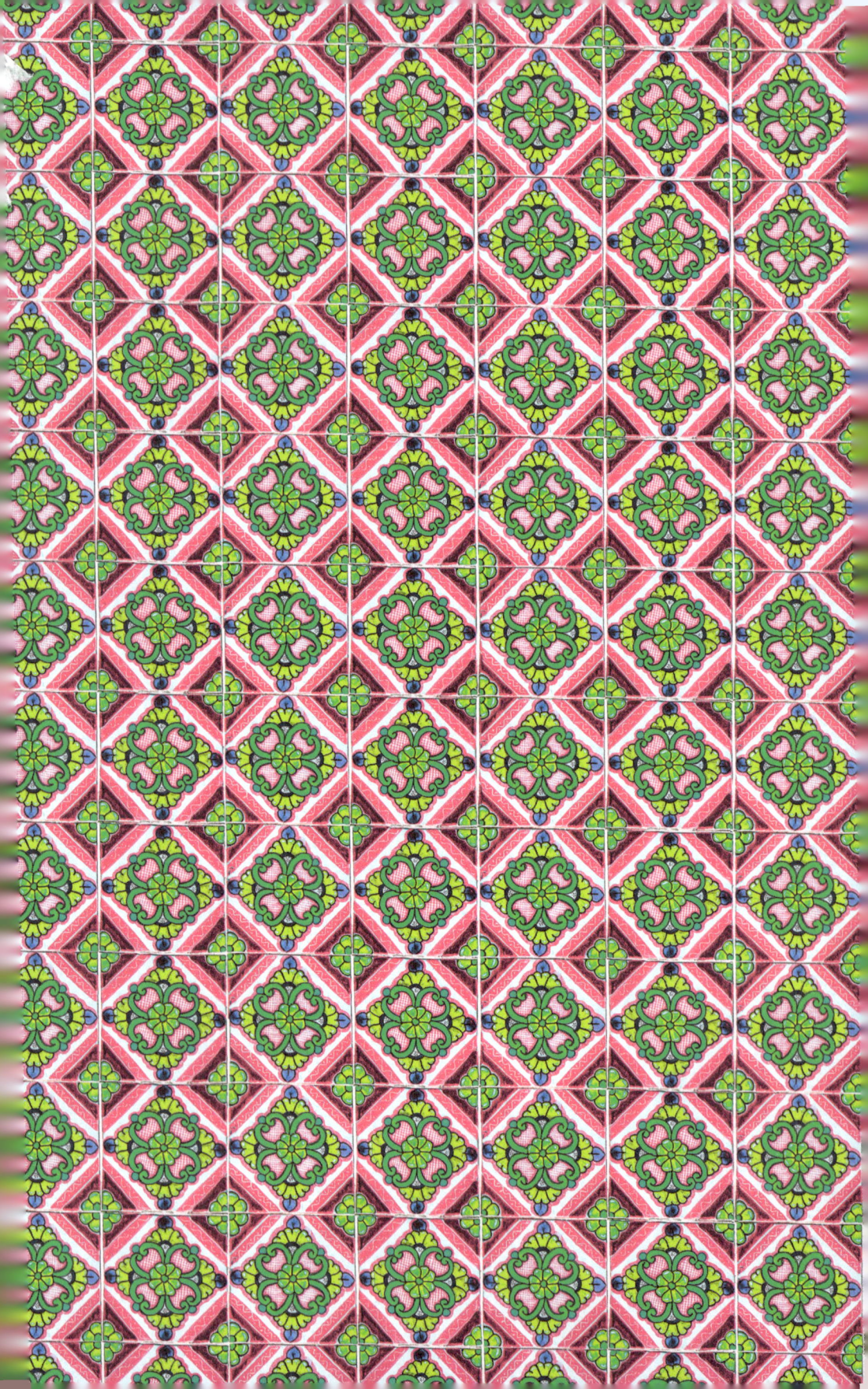

CONTENTS

Prologue

Part 1

NAKED BUT CLOTHED

1. Introduction 5
2. In the Beginning: Eve's Story 13

Part 2

WHAT ARE YOU WEARING?

3. Who Dressed You Today? 21
4. The Garment of Shame 27
5. Ripping Off Rejection 31
6. Shaking Off Fear 35
7. Dressed in Disappointment 39
8. The Garment of Grief 43
9. The Bandaid of Bitterness 49
10. The Fig Leaf of Performance 55

11. The Fig Leaf of Male Attention 59

12. Fig Leaves of All Kinds 63

Part 3

THE GREAT EXCHANGE

13. A Love Story 69

14. The Wardrobe at The Foot of the Cross 75

15. The Currency of Heaven 81

16. The Daily Exchange 85

17. Clothing One Another 89

Part 4

PUT ON YOUR BEAUTIFUL GARMENTS

18. Awake, Awake 95

19. Put on Your Beautiful Garments 101

20. Dressed in Salvation 105

21. The Robe of Righteousness 111

22. Clothed in Strength 117

23. Dressed in Dignity 123

24. The Adornment of Peace 129

25. Clothed in Joy 137

26. The Garment of Praise 145

27. The Belt of Truth 151

28. Clothed in Compassion 157

29. Clothed in Kindness 163

30. The Garment of Humility 169

31. Graced with Gentleness 173

32. Clothed in Patience 177

33. Layers of Love 185

34. Clothed in Power 193

35. Crowned with Beauty 197

Part 5

DRESSED FOR DESTINY

36. Shake Off The Dust 203

37. Sit Enthroned 207

38. Back to the Garden 213

39. Daughters in Training 219

40. Paths of Purpose 223

NAKED BUT CLOTHED

Naked, beautiful and perfectly made,
She stands in the garden unafraid,
Covered by glory, freedom, and love,
Pinnacle of creation, adored from above,

Choice designed by the Maker's hand,
Preyed on by darkness in the land,
And this beauty created to rule and reign,
Breaks trust and now is covered in shame.

Desperate to cover creation flawed,
Fig leaves upon the form adored,
Heartbroken, He knows her leaves will break.
Her shame, her darkness He must take.

And in His pain, He reaches down,
And pierces His heart to form her gown,
Leaves are gone, and clothing is born,
Beauty redeemed for her heavenly form.

Part One

NAKED BUT CLOTHED

Chapter One

INTRODUCTION

It was the end of the summer holidays and I was exhausted and terrified, looking down the barrel of another year of challenge and trial.

I am a mum to three high-energy, beautiful, bold, loving and strong-willed boys. Some families have one strong-willed child, maybe two. In my family, it is all three. I am the mother with the shopping trolley with four wheels that have a mind of their own, trying to negotiate the aisles of a fully-stacked life.

I also have one high-energy, lovingly enthusiastic, super passionate, bi-vocational husband. When the Lord ordained this poetry-writing introvert to marry the world's most social, party-loving, businessman and pastor, heaven giggled. And I sweetly smiled and battered my eyes, naïve to the wild ride I was embarking upon.

In addition to this family of men, big and little, we carry in our heart and hands one vibrant, colourful and very alive church in the heart of downtown Sydney. God In The City (also known as C3 Church City) has been a labour of love for my husband and I since we first dated in the year 2000. Sometimes it is a harvest field of joy and celebration, and sometimes it's a harvest field of strain, weeping and tears.

Prior to marriage, motherhood and ministry, I was a young Sydney lawyer. Graduating from Sydney University Law School with honours was a breeze compared to the steep learning curve of marriage, motherhood and ministry.

These three Ms (marriage, motherhood and ministry) reduced me to a lump of clay on a spinning wheel at the mercy of the potter's hands.

In the summer of 2014, in addition to my busy boys, bouncy husband and bubbly church, we were managing two house moves brought on by the Global Financial Crisis and several behind-the-scenes personal battles. I was one eager-to-please-everyone, good girl, breaking under the strain of it all.

I am not a girl for whom tears come quickly. They arrive at random moments and unexpected places.

This time it was a movie that reached into my heart and pierced the bubble of tears waiting to be shed.

Sometimes there's no time for tears. Life goes on, boys need my care and it feels like God needs my constant strength and support to keep His show on the road.

So, this particular night, I did what all good Christians and responsible wives and mothers do. I picked up my latest self-development book and tried to pull myself together. Who doesn't want to be 'together' for this gig called life?

That's when I heard His voice. The only sound I know with pure love through every chord of its tone. The voice that knows me inside and out. The one that knows about all the mess and yet calls me out through it all.

'Kirrily, put the book down,' the Spirit of God whispered to my heart.

I slowly lowered the book from my face, trusting that voice, but also knowing the mess that lay behind the pages. I was broken. My heart was fragmented. The tears flowed, and my heart collapsed in pieces, incapable of holding it all together for another year.

I don't feel beautiful when life breaks me. I don't feel beautiful when I'm messy. But on this night, I discovered that there is one who finds me beautiful when I'm broken.

There is one who can handle the mess. One who loves Kirrily the messy.

Not Kirrily the perfect.

Not Kirrily the performer.

Not Kirrily the good girl.

But Kirrily the messy.

That voice again.

'I love Kirrily messy. I love broken Kirrily. Come to me naked. Come to me as you are and let me see the real you. Take away the masks. Don't try to patch it all together, come to me vulnerable and broken.'

And so, I came to Him.

The tears flowed and brokenness was exposed. My sense of incapability for living the life He had called me to was bare before Him. Yet, His perfect love washed through it all. His beautiful, light, believing face held His gaze of love as I broke.

And in that place of acceptance and love of my broken form, I fell asleep.

And then it was morning.

Still broken, bewildered, and loved up from the night before, I stumbled out to the lounge room to find God's Word and set my feet upon the Rock for the day that was to come.

I was perplexed before my Creator.

For though I heard His voice inviting me to take off the masks, the broken form underneath was in no position to take on the world.

Though our God may love broken and messy, I was not sure that the staff at church wanted their pastor broken and messy.

So, I found myself in a dilemma.

How do we do broken and messy, and bold and powerful all at once?

How do we do vulnerable and robust?

How do we do naked but clothed?

God loved me broken, but the world needed me bold. Vulnerability is good, but my life requires my strength. God loves me heart-naked, but the world requires me heart-clothed.

So, my journal entry that morning became my inquiry, and my answer, and the foundation of this book:

Lord, I come before you this morning, feeling a bit broken, messy, and smashed. Do you know what is wild? Even broken, you still require obedience and faith. You call us to walk out on your Word and believe what you have said about us.

So, heart raw, aware of my inadequacies and failures, you call me to stand on what you say — who you say I am.

As I take off masks of performance, masks that lead to fear, anxiety, and comparison, I ask you to clothe me with your words and with your truth.

Lord, what is the difference between the masks that we put on and the clothing/armour that you give us? What is the difference between covering and clothing?

I sense the masks that we put on are all built by human hands; they are fashioned by our own doing. They are our idea of what is acceptable to you. They are clothes that we make to cover ourselves before you.

The problem is they have never cut it. Right back in the garden, Adam and Eve did it first. They realised their nakedness and fashioned garments from fig leaves, and they hid; they hid their nakedness from you.

I love what you did. You didn't leave them naked.

After the Fall, the human condition became fractured and needed a covering. We need to be clothed, but we are unable to clothe ourselves. Our garments are makeshift and flimsy and are not pleasing to you.

So, you make them garments of leather. You slaughter the first animal, and with a breaking heart you clothe the man and woman that you love, the man and woman you walk with, the man and woman you created.

Then at the Cross, the body of your heavenly Son was broken. His perfect life stripped to clothe the nakedness of humanity's flesh. His divinity covering our broken and shattered heart. Our nakedness clothed.

So today, I take off my makeshift garments, loosely sewn and trying to hold it all together. I put on your mighty clothing of light and righteousness. I put on boldness, strength, and victory, and I walk with you. You know my heart, you know my frame, yet you clothe me in the wardrobe of your Son, and send me out.

As I wrote, I understood. Christ calls us to Himself broken, vulnerable, and messy. Then He takes of Himself, of His own life, and He clothes us with Himself; with strength, victory, boldness, and power.

That morning I put on garments that were His, but as His daughter they are also mine. I put on strength, boldness, authority and power, and I went to work. I pastored, clothed in Him. I led in His strength and not my own.

Then over the coming months, I sensed that the Lord was entrusting me with a message that was not just for me, but for all the broken, beautiful, messy, and radically-loved girls out there.

If you are reading this book, it is highly likely that you are one of them.

Adored by your Creator and Lord, yet carrying what Ann Voskamp calls *'the unspoken broken"*. [1]

You know you are on the planet for a purpose that is poignant, beautiful, and powerful, yet you might be feeling a little too messy, troubled, and complicated to pull it off.

Perhaps as you read this, the Lord is asking you to take off the mask and let Him love you. Let Him love you naked. Let Him love you through the tears. Let Him see you. Allow the author of love to accept you through and through.

Then, let Him clothe you. Let Him unveil His heavenly wardrobe to clothe your broken form.

Learn to take from His life and wear it as your own.

Dress your vulnerability in Christ's translucent beauty, enhancing the light within, instead of covering it with our own hard masks.

After all, the author of all creation said it Himself at the end of His book:

> *'Buy your clothes from me, clothes designed in heaven. You've walked around half-naked long enough'*
> Revelation 3:18 MSG

So, let's walk together through His heavenly wardrobe.

Let's look to heaven when it seems there is no outfit for the real you, and let's discover a wardrobe that is out of this world.

A wardrobe designed in heaven for you. A wardrobe designed for the woman on the inside, THE INVISIBLE SHE.

You will notice internal clothes that you may be wearing just don't seem like you anymore.

You may discover they don't fit properly.

Or you may decide you cannot stand them any longer, and it's time for a complete change.

Let's do a wardrobe makeover together.

IN THE BEGINNING:
EVE'S STORY

To understand our story as women, we need to start at the beginning. Right back to the mother of all living. To Eve, the beautiful life spring of creation.

In the beginning, she was naked, and she was beautiful.

Comfortable and confident in her identity. Bold and beautiful before her Creator.

She had no need for clothing, for there was nothing to cover.

Beautiful inside and out, she took her place of dominion on the earth.

Then the lies started, whispered by a creature that slithered along the ground.

> Now the serpent was more crafty than any of the wild animals the Lord God had made. He said to the woman, "Did God really say, 'You must not eat from any tree in the garden'?"
>
> The woman said to the serpent, "We may eat fruit from the trees in the garden, but God did say, 'You must not eat fruit from the tree that is in the middle of the garden, and you must not touch it, or you will die.'"
>
> "You will not certainly die," the serpent said to the woman.
> "For God knows that when you eat from it, your eyes will be opened, and you will be like God, knowing good and evil." When the woman saw that the fruit of the tree was good for food and pleasing to the eye, and also desirable for gaining wisdom, she took some and ate it. She also gave some to her husband, who was with her, and he ate it. Then the eyes of both of them were opened, and they realised they were

naked; so they sewed fig leaves together and made coverings for themselves.
Genesis 3:1-7

In effect, the serpent whispered,

> 'There is more Eve. Who you are and what you have is not enough. There is more.'

Then Eve, wooed by the slithering voice on the ground, shifted her ears from the sound of heaven. **She rejected the perfection and completion of who she already was to be something different.** She took her value into her own hands and rejected the inherent worth her Father had already assigned.

She believed the lie that there was more. More than the magnificent creation that she already was. She ate, and the nakedness she was so comfortable in was shattered by the lie of not-enough. Her reality became her shame.

Her quest to be more than what God created her to be broke her heart and pierced her soul.

Eve's battle became our battle.

Believing that who we are is not enough, like Eve, we make choices that break and fracture the beauty on the inside of us.

When Adam and Eve broke unity and trust with their Creator, they realised their nakedness and reached for fig leaves. Bodies bathed in sunlight became bodies covered by leaves. Shame-laced vulnerability caused them to hide in the very garden created for them to rule and reign within.

Today, humanity has its own sets of fig leaves. Some basic, simple and obvious, and some highly sophisticated and sewn together over years of trying to hide our broken spaces.

Sometimes we think relationships, like the love of a man or a woman, will cover our brokenness.

For some of us it's drugs, or alcohol or other addictions.

Or, we use fig leaves a little harder to identify, like career success, the approval of people, performance addiction or obsessive control.

But these coverings are weak. They break and leave us floundering and naked once again. Patching our brokenness with things of earth leaves us vulnerable and exposed.

Even as Christians, we have our own set of fig leaves. Leaves like performance and perfectionism.

Religion itself, when focused on rules and rituals at the expense of a genuine relationship with the Spirit of God, is a fig leaf used by men and women to cover their broken form.

Perhaps you are hiding behind a role — the perfect wife, the excellent housekeeper, the stoic single Mum, the angry activist, the self-made career woman, or even ministry success.

It is a good thing to strive for excellence, but not at the expense of being real. Not at the cost of an authentic and genuine relationship with the God of the universe.

Ignorant of the clothes of heaven, we seek the fig leaves of this earth.

The problem with fig leaves is they hide us from God, and they hide us from each other.

They cover our true beauty and never enhance it. They are makeshift, flimsy and fragile and not pleasing to God.

In the garden, our passionate and purposeful Creator took the matter into His own hands.

Looking upon our brokenness, He broke the body of an animal and shed its skin to form our clothes. Adam and Eve tenderly clothed by their Maker.

At the cross, the body of His heavenly Son was broken. His life was stripped to clothe the nakedness of the human soul.

There is provision, there is heavenly provision.

His seamless robe of life was shed and divided among us. (John 19:23-24)

In the garden, it was leather.

Today it is His life, His beauty, His perfection to clothe, redeem, and make beautiful our naked form.

In the last book of the Bible, we are reminded of His provision from the beginning:

> *'Buy your clothes from me, clothes designed in heaven.
> You've gone around half-naked long enough. And buy medicine
> for your eyes from me so you can see, really see.'*
> Revelation 3:18 MSG

Our eyes need medicine to see the heavenly wardrobe, the divine provision.

In the garden, the eyes of Adam and Eve were opened to their naked form.

Today we need the heavenly medicine of God's Word to open our eyes to the seamless clothing of the life of Christ.

For it is the strategy of the enemy to cover the beauty of a woman.

It is the intent of heaven to clothe a woman and put her beauty on display.

Yes, it was God's initial intent that we were naked before Him. It is His redemptive intent that we are clothed by Him.

> For when darkness thought it had its way,
> Our Maker heralds a brand-new day.
> With provision for our broken form,
> Beauty enhanced as He adorns.
>
> And so we wake to a new command,
> To take from His wardrobe and take our stand.
> And in the last book, He makes himself clear,
> Strip off your fig leaves, your clothing is here.
>
> The words are spoken, 'Buy your clothes from me.'
> 'Clothes designed in heaven.' Open eyes to see.

Part Two

WHO DRESSED YOU TODAY?

Chapter Three

WHO DRESSED YOU TODAY?

Who dressed you today?

I don't mean the clothes on the outside. Although it is worth considering whether you dressed yourself or allowed the latest fashion craze to clothe you in something that doesn't suit you at all.

But that aside, **who dressed you on the inside?**

So often we are wearing internal garments we never chose, garments cast over us by others or by circumstance.

Often we are wearing an inner wardrobe that no longer fits. Possibly garments that should have been discarded long ago. Garments we just accepted, because we didn't understand we had an option.

Some of us have watched our parents, teachers or friends put on beautiful internal garments and we have learnt to do the same.

This is a good thing.

As a young girl, I learnt to wear the garment of kindness as my Mum taught me to treat others the way that I would like to be treated.

But some of us have watched others model a terrible wardrobe, and we have learnt to dress the same.

We fail to realise that we can choose what we wear on the inside.

I remember the moment I realised that I had a choice. I was in my early twenties, smothered under garments that were blocking the light.

I adored my Dad, but some aspects of his life were yet to be redeemed.

There were patterns of negativity and criticism, born from challenges in his own life, that were clothing and ultimately suffocating me.

The clothes of others in our family can quickly become our own.

As a child, the choices of those around us can be all that we know, and their clothes can become our wardrobe.

Some of these clothes can be great, but some are not.

As a young adult, darkness had set in under a hereditary patchwork of negativity in my life. It was a garment that didn't fit me, didn't become me. It was a garment I couldn't live in, breathe in or move in.

The moment I realised I didn't have to wear this garment was a moment of pure liberation.

Family patterns that are not healthy do not need to define us. Each of us has the opportunity to choose our own internal wardrobe.

There are many valuable and beautiful garments I inherited from my family. But I have decided to throw off the ones that are not so becoming, that don't match the woman that God has created me to be.

Some of the clothes you are wearing may have been picked up as a child, but sometimes, it is as recent as last year, last month, or yesterday.

How easy it is to wear rejection when you have been hurt by a friend.

How easy it is to wear shame when you have made a mistake.

Or disappointment when you have been let down.

How easy it is to wear grief for years after loss, or bitterness for decades after we have been wronged.

I have been sharing this message with women for over a decade, across many different churches and nations.

After speaking, I always extend an invitation to women to change their wardrobe. There is never a time when the altar is not full of women engaging in this wardrobe change.

I have heard stories of women wearing the words of teachers from twenty years ago.

I have prayed for grandmothers wearing the rejection of an adult child. I have talked with wives who are wearing the hurt of mistreatment by their husbands and choose to put on dignity instead. I have met adult children wearing the expectations of parents, and many realising that fear has become a garment suffocating their lives.

I pray that as you read this book, your eyes will be opened to the clothes that you are wearing that may not become you, and like me, you can make the decision to throw them off.

Sometimes the decision is instantaneous, and the garment is cast off. But sometimes it can be progressive, slow and painful to strip off outfits that are so familiar they are almost entwined with who you are.

The more we open our eyes to our wardrobe in God's Word, the more we become aware of the ill-fitting outfits that clothe us, and the more we are inclined to strip them off.

What we wear on the inside matters. More important than being dressed for success on the outside, is choosing to dress for success on the inside.

Recently the first all-female spacewalk was scheduled, where two women would venture outside of their space station on a six-hour mission to install batteries. This potentially historic moment fell through because they did not have the right sized spacesuit for the second female, so her male counterpart replaced her.[2] She did not have the right wardrobe, and therefore missed this moment in history.

Are you dressed right for your mission?

Or are you wearing old clothes that are covering and blocking the real you? Clothes that are dragging you down, causing you to trip and miss opportunities and appointments prepared for you?

There is an internal wardrobe that will either compromise or enhance our opportunities in life.

It is so much more important to have our inner wardrobe sorted, yet so little emphasis is put on this in the world we live in.

There are garments that will set you up for success. Garments like strength, grace, compassion, kindness, dignity, love, courage and humility.

How much more effective could our life's journey be if we were dressed well on the inside?

Steven Furtick, a great preacher, once said, *'Unless lies are exposed, callings will never be fulfilled.'* [3]

I would say that unless certain garments are ripped off and replaced with others, some dreams will never be realised.

The wardrobe within matters. Who would have thought a woman's spacewalk mission could be cancelled because of an outfit?

Is your spacesuit ready? Have you accessed the heavenly garments needed for a heavenly mission?

Have you stripped off the old to put on the new?

The following pages explain some of the inner garments I realised I was wearing and my journey of stripping them off. They are garments that no doubt caused the cancelling of several missions. They were certainly not the spacesuit needed to land on the moon, or the new creation identity required to fulfil my purpose in Christ.

Perhaps you will find yourself in these pages, or maybe you will become aware of other ill-fitting garments you have on.

Whatever heavy garments or flimsy fig leaves are covering you, I'm praying that as you read the rest of this book, you'll start to recognise them and strip them off.

Chapter Four

THE GARMENT OF SHAME

Shame has this way of subtly being cast over our life without us realising it. It has the ability to weave itself through our everyday garments. It's thread discolouring, polluting and entangling our world.

Shame is not the feeling that we did something wrong, or someone did something wrong to us. It is the belief that we are wrong, there is something wrong with us, that we are fundamentally flawed.

Shame is a dead-end road, and it is the very antithesis of the truth, hope and redemption revealed in the Gospel.

Like every dark and ill-fitting garment that seeks to cover the beauty and colour of who we are, **shame gains its access through lies.**

The enemy of our soul lies to us in a moment of failure or sin.[4] Or perhaps the lie takes root in the event of abuse, neglect, mistreatment, or rejection by others. The lie is that there is something wrong with us. That we are intrinsically unloveable and fundamentally flawed.

He offers us the dark cloak of shame, and often unknowingly we take it and put it on, thinking it will hide us and cover us. We assume we have no choice but to wear this dark garment and believe the lie that it is part of who we are.

And yes, it does hide us and cover us. It envelops us and shields us from the light—from the light of truth and freedom. It shields us from others, from healing, from community, from love and from acceptance.

This cloak is also long, and it trips us up as we take steps forward.

I didn't even realise what I was wearing. Like many other children of alcoholics, shame was such an intrinsic part of my identity, I didn't realise it was possible to feel differently. It was a dark garment of knowing that my family had a dysfunction that others didn't. A garment of deep shame placed on me by the lifestyle choice of my beloved Dad.

My Dad grew up in a pub, to wonderful and loving but very busy parents. At the age of six he was sent to boarding school. Until the time of his passing, he still had nightmares of his time as a young boy at that strict Catholic boys boarding school. In his mid-teens, he shifted to a day school and went wild with freedom, parties and girls.

Unlike his brothers who went on to university and became lawyers, my Dad found himself in the world of nightclubs, parties and fun. The liquor industry seemed a natural fit, and after settling down somewhat with Mum, he purchased bottle shops to support a growing family.

It seemed natural that a bottle shop owner would wind down each night with some beers and a bottle of wine. But Dad would shift during those times from pleasant and reasonable to unpleasant and difficult to be around. Thankfully, my dad changed significantly in the last five to ten years of his life. But the impact of his lifestyle had a significant impact upon me as a young woman.

Without understanding it, shame had become part of my identity.

I remember the moment I stripped shame off. I remember the flood of light. The wave of freedom. The outpouring of unconditional love, acceptance, righteousness and power.

I was twenty-four, and I realised that the negative aspects of my upbringing could not define who I was. The only one with the power to define my identity, was the one who created me, who birthed me into existence, who ordained my days and prepared my future. I stripped off shame and stepped into truth, freedom and authority.

But, oh how that garment loves to throw itself over us again and again. When trouble or challenge comes, the enemy offers the cloak and says, 'It's your fault, it's because of you, there is something wrong with you.'

The worst thing is when we don't even recognise the lie. We just wear the thoughts that come, or the words others throw on us, and fail to choose our own wardrobe.

I try not to accept the latest fashion trends just because. I wear clothes that I love, clothes that suit me, not the clothes that society defines as cool at one point in time.

In fact, for about two or three years, I rebelled against wearing skinny-leg jeans. Not only did I find them uncomfortable during a particularly stressful season in my life, but the fact that they seemed an essential wardrobe item for every female preacher totally irritated me.

I like dresses: beautiful dresses, unique dresses, long dresses, colourful dresses, patterned dresses, floral dresses, intricate dresses. Dresses that bring beauty into a house of much testosterone.

We must learn to choose our own wardrobe. I would not accept a garment thrown over me by just anyone. Only by someone who loves me, knows me, recognises the uniqueness of who I am, and chooses clothes accordingly.

It is the same spiritually. So many of us wear whatever garment is cast on us—rejection, shame, unworthiness. We walk around with ill-fitting clothes, not realising that we have power over our own wardrobe.

Shame is never handed to us by our Creator. In fact, it is quite the opposite—He is intent on taking it away and replacing it with His radiance. So, I look to Him again today, and dress from His custom-made wardrobe full of beauty and grace.

Shame is left on the floor, with all the other lies and half-truths, and I step out clothed in the truth found in His Word and radiant in the reflection of the Son; clothed in Him. I dress in His love and the honour He bestows upon me as His daughter.

Clothed in honour, I am transformed, made radiant by His love.

'Those who look to him are radiant; their faces are never covered in shame'
Psalm 34:5

Chapter Five

RIPPING OFF REJECTION

There is one garment that is so painful it takes our breath away.

When we wear it, tears seep out of the side of who we are, our breath is sharp, and the pain is acute.

We've all known it.

It's painful because we weren't created to wear it.

It is sharp, hard, abrasive, light-blocking and heavy.

It's the garment of rejection. The very word brings tears to my eyes, as it does to the God who made you for full acceptance, for celebration, for community.

Are you wearing it today? Where are you wearing it?

Is it on your feet - stopping you from walking into God-given appointments? Is it on your hands, stopping your creativity?

Is it in your mind, seeping through neural pathways, whispering that you are unloved and unlovable? Maybe it's over your heart, preventing you from loving or letting anyone in.

I can feel it trying to take over my wardrobe, trying to infect every item of clothing with its touch. Like a disease, it's hard to stop its spread. It will take over until you are trapped in darkness, pain and confusion.

We can rip at this garment with positive thinking, the acceptance of another, the acceptance of achievement, performance, good works. But it grows back.

How do we shed this garment? How do we get rid of it once and for all?

There is only one place.

Freedom from rejection has always been, and will always be, found **at the foot of the Cross**.

The Cross that performs the mystery all humanity has cried out for. 'Free me from these garments that are not who I really am!'

And at the Cross, He took them.

In one violent *'not my will, but yours'*[5], the Saviour of humanity violently ripped out every thread of rejection that wove its way through the human condition.

Christ bore the ultimate rejection when he cried out "My God, my God, *why have you forsaken me?"*[6]. Rejected in a moment of torturous anguish by His own heavenly Father, so we could be embraced.

Sometimes we forget the rejection Christ bore. Misunderstood by His own family,[7] rejected by the nation he was born into, betrayed by the disciples He loved and murdered by the people He came to save. Ultimately sacrificed outside the city gate,[8] to make way for all found outside the gate. To open a new gate. A gate for the rejected, the outcast, the lonely and the despised. A gate of acceptance into the unconditional love of a heavenly Father.

And this is where the thread of rejection is undone. It unravels in the mystery, wonder and power of the perfect sacrifice.

It lays powerless on the ground, and there we are naked, in all our human brokenness before the One whose love accepts us, transforms us, and clothes us.

His love and His sacrifice make a new weave, and this weave creates a new garment—a garment of infinite worth, beauty and delicate wonder.

It's available for everyone who stands at the foot of the Cross and lets the Saviour of the world rip away rejection.

It is His own garment, created and bestowed by the Father. It is the garment of sonship, of daughtership, of belonging, of 'you're mine'.

RIPPING OFF REJECTION

Come daily to my store,
And wear what I once wore,
I'll take away the threads,
And the thoughts inside your head.

For the sting of betrayal,
Won't ring the final bell,
They forget the great exchange,
The final rearrange.

Where rejection bows it's head,
To the One who'll raise the dead,
And acceptance is the song,
That will finish which was wrong.

Chapter Six

SHAKING OFF FEAR

The feeling is familiar.

It creeps up through my lungs, grips my heart, distorts my thoughts, and I start to feel myself retreat in fear.

I retreat from what I know is true, retreat from the ones I love. I withdraw from my purpose, hide under the covers.

The feeling is fear.

Unfortunately, it is too recognisable. It almost feels like a part of me, like truth, like who I am.

I suspect I picked it up as a little girl, even as a babe in the womb. My beautiful mum grew up in an era where women wore worry as a virtue. Worry was woven through my form, as an essential weave of everyday life.

However, worry unchecked becomes the breeding ground of fear, and fear unchecked becomes a force that will straight-jacket our lives.

Most of us have been touched by fear.

It weaves itself around our breath like a snake. Whispering half-truths. Magnifying giants. Twisting our thoughts. Sinking its poison into our lungs, taking away our very breath and life.

Some of us are more vulnerable to it than others. Some of us haven't been trained to recognise and resist its slithery lies.

I was one of the vulnerable ones.

Until recently, until now. Now it is different. There is another force inside of me that hates this snake.

The snake still slithers, continuing its attempts to disguise its poison as truth. My flesh wants to retreat under its power. To run, to hide.

But I know too much now. Truth has woven its way through the fabric of my being like stitches holding me together, not pulling me apart.

And this truth, these beautiful stitches, stand like soldiers, strong against the lies. The truth whispers, "fear not, stand up, rise and shine, be not afraid, keep walking."

I am no longer one of the fearful ones. I can no longer yield to its lies.

I am a brave heart. Descended from the bravest one of all.

His nature resides on the inside of me, and I must stand.

I must stand against fear, stand against the lies that slither around my heart and mind, stand against the parts of me that want to run, want to hide, want to retreat. I am not that person anymore.

I begin to stand up in all that I know is true.

A crown rests on my head as I stand.

Courage is the countenance of the Kingdom.

It fits us well.

It lifts us up rather than pushes us down. Draws us out rather than pokes us in.

I begin to peel off the snake, strip off its constricting grip.

I remember my cloak of courage. And I put it on.

You have to stand up to put on this garment.

It is not a garment to be worn sitting down.

It fits me perfectly. I feel like myself again. Not my old self, but my ancient self, created in the heavenly realm before the foundations of the world. A new nature, this time a nature that fits.

A brave one. A bold one. Created with courage for our brave new world.

Chapter Seven

DRESSED IN DISAPPOINTMENT

Some garments are simply too heavy to wear.

Weighty, ill-fitting and dark. Blocking joy.

Shutting out the light. Weighing us down.

We are not designed for certain weights; they are crushing to our soul.

I recognise a weight on my own heart as the garment of disappointment.

It needs to go so I can breathe, so I can run, so I can wear His yoke. [9]

That is the challenge with disappointment. The heart can carry little else when carrying this heavy weight.

Sometimes we are sailing in one direction, with all our hopes and dreams focused on a specific destination when life suddenly changes course. We hit a wall, or a large bolted closed door, or a storm we cannot pass, and we need to change direction.

In a moment, our life turns and heads a completely different way.

But, oh, how our hearts are slow to change! They long for the old, they get stuck in the dreams of a different day.

Stuck under disappointment, stuck in broken dreams.

I remember the story of Peter, stuck under a heavy load of his own. Stuck in the disappointment of His own failings, His own shortcomings.

He was so keen to do good, to be brave, to follow Jesus at all costs, but so human, just like us. Christ was painfully aware of Peter's frailty, yet nonetheless grafted him into His plan.

Then Jesus told them,

> "This very night you will all fall away on account of me, for it is written: "'I will strike the shepherd, and the sheep of the flock will be scattered.' But after I have risen, I will go ahead of you into Galilee." Peter replied, "Even if all fall away on account of you, I never will." "Truly I tell you," Jesus answered, "this very night, before the rooster crows, you will disown me three times."
> But Peter declared, "Even if I have to die with you, I will never disown you." And all the other disciples said the same.
> Matthew 26:31-35

Peter crumbled, failed under pressure and denied His Saviour and Lord. Covered in shame, broken commitments and shattered dreams.

> With a shattered heart, Peter went out of the courtyard, sobbing with bitter tears.
> Matthew 26:75 TPT

But Peter didn't allow his regret, grief and disappointment in himself to keep him from God's people and ultimately from His Lord.

> 'Then the disciple whom Jesus loved said to Peter, "It is the Lord!" As soon as Simon Peter heard him say, "It is the Lord," he wrapped his outer garment around him (for he had taken it off) and jumped into the water.'
> John 21:7

Peter didn't waste any time running (or in this case, swimming) to the Lord. Sometimes our disappointment can keep us from God, but I encourage you to run to Him, swim to Him, and jump into His arms with your disappointment. He is the Healer and the One who strips off the heavy garments that weigh us down.

Peter swam to the One who rolls rocks away. He swam to Jesus, who once was buried in a tomb of His own and caused the stone to roll away.

The Bible says the angels sat on that stone. They sat on it. The rock meant to block the eternal light from humankind was shifted and used as a seat.

Peter, with his own burden, ran to the One who moved the stone.

And the stone shifter, with words of power, shifted the stone from Peter's heart.

Sometimes it is only Jesus who can move the stone of disappointment; who, with resurrection life, can re-awaken our spirit with the words of His appointment.

> *When they had finished eating, Jesus said to Simon Peter,*
> *"Simon son of John, do you love me more than these?"*
> *"Yes, Lord," he said, "you know that I love you." Jesus said,*
> *"Feed my lambs." Again Jesus said, "Simon son of John, do you*
> *love me?" He answered, "Yes, Lord, you know that I love you."*
> *Jesus said, "Take care of my sheep." The third time he said to him,*
> *"Simon son of John, do you love me?"*
> *Peter was hurt because Jesus asked him the third time,*
> *"Do you love me?" He said, "Lord, you know all things;*
> *you know that I love you." Jesus said, "Feed my sheep."*
> *John 21:15-17*

Three times Peter denied Christ, and three times the Lord affirmed Peter's calling. Three times displacing disappointment with a new appointment.

Disappointment displaced by a Jesus appointment.

The heavy garment of disappointment is stripped off and exchanged with the light-filled wonder of a God-given mantle, a Jesus appointment.

We run into the arms of Jesus with our weighty garments of disappointment, and we allow Him to replace them with the energy and lightness of His commissioning.

In the words of Joyce Meyer, the question is not **'why God, why?'**, but **'what now God?'**[10]

Let His appointment displace disappointment.

Chapter Eight

THE GARMENT OF GRIEF

There are times in life when loss is so painful that grief can rest with us for days, months and years. Unprocessed grief begins to clothe us, a dark garment of mourning that becomes part of our spiritual wardrobe.

In our fallen world, loss is part of our lives. However, loss is not something that our human frames were created to carry long term. We were designed for a garden of eternal life that knew no loss, no pain, no decay. Instead, we find ourselves in a world with death, decay, war, conflict and broken relationships.

When loss visits our heart and our home, the pain can be deep and complex and can mark the beginning of a long journey of letting go.

But some of us get stuck on the journey of grief, trapped and suffocating under the heavy garment of mourning that just will not seem to shift.

Grief was never designed as a garment, but rather a journey. A journey of profoundly feeling the pain of loss and then engaging in the great exchange. Trusting the Great I Am with His sovereign plan. Allowing a Saviour who suffered, to take the pain. Then finally facing with courage and hope, a day that is new and different.

To be healthy, grief must be a journey and not a gown. A verb, rather than a noun.

Jesus was acquainted with grief but anointed with joy.

This is the One that I follow.

I have found the garment of grief hard to strip off on my own.

I have needed companions to walk with me through the various valleys of the shadow of death my journey has taken me through. Companions who have gently encouraged me to keep walking when I want to sit, stop and sleep in the valley. I have needed companions to encourage me to grieve but not wear grief, and there is a big difference.

Maybe as you read, you recognise a garment of grief. Allow me to come alongside you in the valley, with the promise that in Christ, death leads to new life. For if you bravely allow Christ to bear your griefs, He will pin that gown of mourning to the Cross that He alone had to endure.

I promise that the beautiful Spirit of Life will birth a garden of beauty and colour on the inside of you.

A garden that will once again give off a sweet aroma to the world around you.

The world is waiting for the transformation inside of you on the other side of grief.

In your journey of transformation, let me introduce you to another valley walker. A woman who transformed grief into something that brought salvation to the earth.

Her name is Ruth, meaning 'friend'. She is a woman who chose to walk through the valley of grief, and birth life on the other side.

Ruth, the Moabitess, was joined to God's people through marriage. Her promise of a future dies with the premature death of her husband. And in her valley, without husband or children, Ruth makes a decision that pastes her onto the pages of God's salvation story.

Ruth chooses to walk with her mother-in-law Naomi, right through the valley of the shadow of death and into the promised land.

In the valley, Ruth makes a declaration of faithfulness that leads her to life.

> *But Ruth replied, "Don't urge me to leave you or to turn back from you. Where you go I will go, and where you stay I will stay. Your people will be my people and your God my God.*
> *Ruth 1:16*

I wonder if we could have the same approach with our Saviour God. Christ walked through great suffering, and even death, to ultimately become the Resurrection and the Life.

What if we understood that walking with Jesus means fellowshipping in His suffering, and joining in His resurrection?

What if we understood that death gives birth to life, mountains border valleys and winter always turns to spring?

So, Ruth walks through the valley and goes out to gather grain in the fields of promise. And her courage transforms her from a grain-gatherer to a mother forming the lineage of the bread of life Himself.

They travelled through the valley to Bethlehem, meaning 'House of Bread', and as she bravely gathered breadcrumbs, she met her kinsmen redeemer and future husband Boaz.

Her grief transformed into a new day. Ruth married Boaz and gave birth to Obed, father of Jesse, father of David, the lineage of King Jesus.

This is the promise ladies, as we choose to bravely allow our King to walk with us through the valley of the shadow of death, we emerge to a new day of promise and redemption.

We throw off the heavy garments of mourning, and we allow the valley of tears to become a place of springs, giving way to newness of life.

> *How enriched are they who find their strength in the Lord;*
> *within their hearts are the highways of holiness!*
> *Even when their paths wind through the dark valley of tears,*
> *they dig deep to find a pleasant pool where others find only pain.*
> *He gives to them a brook of blessing*
> *filled from the rain of an outpouring.*
> *They grow stronger and stronger with every step forward,*
> *and the God of all gods will appear before them in Zion.*
> *Psalm 84:5-7 TPT*

VALLEY VIEW

Seasons of abundance and seasons of pain,
Seasons of death then seasons of gain.
Seasons of richness and seasons of lack,
Seasons of colour and seasons of black.

Seasons where life is swallowed by loss,
Our world transformed at heart-piercing cost.
But what if loss birthed something new,
What if the valley opened our view?

Into a space where our heart grows large,
And Christ is birthed and placed in charge.
What if grief transforms our soul,
Into a garden instead of a hole?

What if grief begins a new day,
Where our broken heart becomes His clay.
For a heart yielded to the Maker's hand
Becomes the fabric of His plans.

He's ever at work weaving the new,
From death to life and all the way through.

Chapter Nine

THE BANDAID OF BITTERNESS

It's a temptation for all of us.

To cover the pain in our hearts with bitterness.

Bitterness toward God. Bitterness toward others. As if maybe this bandaid of bitterness, blame, accusation and anger will somehow hold together the festering pain on the inside of us.

And yet the pain continues, our wounds cry out, and the ones who offended us are powerless to bring the healing. Because like us, they are clothed in flesh, in desperate need of a supernatural God.

I have heard it said about trauma that we are not responsible for what happened to us, but we are responsible for the healing. We so often want to make someone else responsible. We want the one who offended us to fix it all up, to make it right, to heal the open wound that is left.

Offence hurts because it is an offence against us. Somewhere along the line, someone broke God's law toward us, and it hurts. We become the offended, the victim of offence.

In Christian circles, I have heard people shame and criticise those who wear offence, like they are the ones with the problem, with the sin, the ones in the wrong.

It seems we have our own form of victim shaming, perhaps blocking our own sense of inadequacy within the Body of Christ.

And I wonder if we need just a little more compassion. I wonder if compassion needs to enlarge our hearts to make room for the suffering.

People wear offence largely because they have been hurt.

We can't fix people's pain, but we can certainly make space for the wounded, show compassion to the hurting, and maybe even break through some glass ceilings so the broken can come to Jesus.

Yet, in the unrelenting paradox of Christianity, there is essential and profound truth in the need for us to strip off offence. There is no getting around the reality that our wounds can't heal until we bravely remove the bandaid of bitterness.

Until we take our hurts to the only One who can truly heal. It is the redemptive truth of an upside-down gospel where a sinless Saviour suffered, and the wounded became the healer of all humanity.

I am aware that these are not always easy words for the wounded to read.

I write as a wounded healer myself, and the ability to write this chapter has come at a deep personal cost. But I promise you, your healing, freedom and beauty is on the other side of the bandaid of bitterness.

In the stunning words of the book of Hebrews:

> *So, we must let go of every wound that has pierced us and the sin we so easily fall into. Then we will be able to run life's marathon race with passion and determination, for the path has been already marked out before us.*
> *Hebrews 12:1 TPT*

WORDS TO THE WOUNDED

Christ was there when the sword pierced your soul.
Crying out to His Father, 'Let this wound make her whole.'
For there's no way to escape the pain of sin and strife,
No way to undo the piercings of the knife.

No way to fix the wrong that's been done,
No way to avoid roads walked by the Son.
Nicodemus couldn't crawl back in the womb,
But the Father opened another room.

A space carved by the wounds of His Son,
A place to renew the damage done.
A room where our spirit once again comes alive,
And the wounds of our Saviour absorb the knife.

And that is where the healing is found,
Wounds inside His wounds, we turn around.
He carries our sin, our suffering and shame,
He bears the hurts, the piercings, the blame.

He carries what we cannot contain.
The sins of the world and all our pain.
So, in faith we let him take the load,
Offence, the crime, the dark episode.

In faith, forgiving what we can't turn around.
So, in His grace, our lives can be found.
And yes, we become more like Him.
Wounded healers, not carriers of sin.

Agents of grace, of mercy, of love.
Divine forgiveness sourced from above.
For this is the place freedom is found,
Bitterness bandaids left on the ground.

Trampled by the shoes of the gospel of peace,
Coming into agreement with the King's release.
And in its place, the aroma of grace.
Not twisted pain contorting our face.

So, come now remove the bandaid with me.
To wear His grace, the gown of the free.

THE FIG LEAF OF PERFORMANCE

There are moments when the truth hits you, and instantly you can see.

Then there are times when truth must be soaked in. When a lie has become entwined into your being without you even knowing—knitted to the fabric of who you are without your conscious permission.

It goes on like a bandaid, or a big engulfing bandage to quickly cover the pain. Then it remains for years embedded into our skin until it feels like it is who we are. It becomes so enmeshed in our identity that we forget who we really are.

But there are moments when the Lord declares it is time to soak. Time for freedom. Time for the embedded bandages to be gently and lovingly removed in an oiled and scented bath of truth.

Some of us call the lies band-aids. Some call them masks.

Last year I began to call them fig leaves. The same fig leaves Adam and Eve stretched out to cover their shame in the first garden.

Fig leaves weren't bad in and of themselves. They formed part of the beautiful garden of God's creation. They were just never meant to cover the glory of humanity.

And there is this one fig leaf—a big and glorified fig leaf. A fig leaf called performance.

So many of us look at it, admire it, desire it.

Then in a moment of brokenness, we grab at it.

We rip it off the tree to cover our broken heart.

I know when I grabbed mine. I was in my mid-teens and there was unspoken pain in my family home. Not having the awareness or the tools to deal with the pain in my heart, I grabbed at the most socially acceptable fig leaf I could find, the fig leaf of performance. I buried myself in my study, until academic success became a covering that was like a bandaid over my unsettled heart. It worked well for many years, until it broke, and I broke right along with it.

I excelled at school, I graduated with honours from Sydney University Law School, I was awarded second place at Bible College. I did all the right things and subconsciously I was set to perform my way right through the Christian life. Until I could not. Until motherhood, marriage and pastoring broke me, and the fig leaf of performance shattered into parts that could no longer be pieced together.

And I just wonder if heaven cheered, as I finally positioned myself to be clothed in Jesus Christ Himself.

After all, it was a fig tree that Jesus cursed when He walked the earth. Mark 11:13 in The Passion Translation reads,

> *'He noticed a leafy fig tree in the distance, so he walked over to see if there was any fruit on it, but there was none – only leaves…'*

It was at that point that Jesus cursed the fig tree. Lots of fig leaves but no real fruit.

We can be covered in beautiful leaves, but the fruit can be absent.

Jesus then walks alongside and curses the tree of performance that has grown on the inside of us.

The fig leaf of performance blocks the light; it covers the truth; it hides beauty, vulnerability and humanity.

It covers, but it doesn't heal.

It momentarily looks good, but the price to keep it on is high.

It will eventually cost you your energy, your joy, your peace, and the unique beauty of who you are.

Performance is not fruitfulness. Fruitfulness is a fruit, not a leaf.

It grows from within; it's not grabbed from without.

Fruitfulness doesn't block our identity; it blossoms from within, from who we are in Christ.

The fig leaf of performance must be removed for fruitfulness to come forth.

It hurts. When a fig leaf is entwined in our nature, there are wounds underneath. Old wounds, raw wounds.

The Lord will only strip the fig leaf when He is intent on healing. When it is time for the raw open wounds to be soothed, cleansed and healed.

Freedom and truth are on the other side of the pain.

Battling to trust Him with my wounds, I allow Him to peel off the fig leaf of performance.

I scream a little, shrink back more than a little, but ultimately surrender to His work.

Now I know there is one tree that won't just cover my wounds, but will absorb my wounds, heal them, transform them. This is not a tree from the first garden, but a tree from the second garden.

The tree of the Cross.

The only tree we are called to run and hide in.

I run in, and I feel its power.

My wounds aren't covered. They are absorbed.

I let go of the leaves, I step out from behind the other trees, and I smell freedom.

Chapter Eleven

THE FIG LEAF OF MALE ATTENTION

A younger reader urged me to include this chapter, based on the battles and bandaids of her generation.

It is also a chapter that I am desperately familiar with. This bandaid was pasted on many pages of my life before I discovered the incredible love and acceptance of the Lord Jesus Christ.

I was in my late teens, and Dad's attention had shifted. For a season his eyes were off his family, and he was caught in other pursuits.

As I explained previously, I had thrown myself into study and academic success. However as soon as Year 12 ended, and the HSC (Higher School Certificate) was completed, I stepped out of my fig leaf of study and was left with an enormous ache.

Like many other teenage girls, I took that ache to one place. To the arms of any guy who would give me attention.

Since the Fall, there is a brokenness in the feminine identity that craves the covering of a male.

In fact, craving the covering and leadership of a male was a specific consequence of the Fall for womankind.

> *To the woman he said, "I will make your pains in childbearing very severe; with painful labor you will give birth to children. Your desire will be for your husband, and he will rule over you."*
> Genesis 3:16

I have pushed out three babies, and I can confirm that there has been some pain involved.

I can also confirm that I have personally experienced the second part of that curse where my desire and craving has been for a man and his leadership.

My broken feminine nature ached for the covering of a man, without understanding that the real covering for my brokenness was found in the person and life of Jesus Christ. So, I went from relationship to relationship seeking to satisfy my desperate desire to be clothed in love. And the love of a man became a fig leaf over my heart.

In its extreme form today, this is outworked as sex addiction. Young person after young person clicks on their Tinder app to provide temporary relief for the ache inside of them.

However, this fig leaf makes us feel even more naked and exposed. So we go there again, seeking to cover our growing awareness of our exposed form, with another partner, another sexual encounter, and more counterfeit love.

I am not saying that there is not a place for beautiful romantic relationships. Obviously, romance has been created by God. It is a gift in the garden.

But like other fig leaves, it is not meant to become our covering.

It is not the place that God has ordained for us to find our identity and our sense of self. Our identity is found looking straight into the face of Jesus. Our value and worth from knowing Him and His unending love for us.

So, I went from fig leaf to fig leaf until I looked up to Jesus and I became clothed in the radiance of His love. I then understood that my answers weren't found in the arms of an earthly man. My whole future is entwined in the arms of a heavenly man.

After my honeymoon with Jesus, staying free of this fig leaf was not easy. Temptation came, loneliness came, and my desperate need of a quick fix flared up.

But as I stood in the truth I had encountered of the radiant love of Christ, I positioned myself for a relationship established on the foundation of who I am in Christ. A relationship based on a foundation of already knowing my worth and value, rather than seeking to find it in the arms of a man.

Unfortunately ladies, Hollywood has done us a disservice in this area, feeding us a diet of romantic love as the ultimate answer to happiness. This is not true. While romantic love can be a blessing and source of joy, it is not the ultimate source of joy.

That place belongs to Jesus Christ alone. It is found in Him alone.

FIG LEAVES OF ALL KINDS

Fig leaves come in many different shapes and sizes.

In the beginning, fig leaves formed a beautiful part of the garden but they were never meant to cover the naked beauty of humanity.

It's the same today. Many things in life can be good in and of themselves. They are there to be enjoyed, but they are not meant to be glued to our identity, hiding the beauty of who we are.

There is nothing wrong with being an incredible mother, or an excellent wife. In fact, these qualities are admirable and to be pursued. The problem is when they become a pursuit that exceeds our pursuit of God or get in the way of our relationship with Him. The problem is when they cover who we really are, and we use them to hide our vulnerability.

The brokenness in humanity grabs for a fig leaf to cover the pain, to hide the wound, to clothe our inadequacy. For some the fig leaf is an addiction to alcohol or drugs or other substances and habits that are used to cover, block and hide. Addictions come in many different shapes and sizes. You may be blocking pain and numbing with pornography, self-harm, cutting, gambling, stealing, TV, movies, Netflix, food, phones, gaming, work, shopping, and the list goes on.

For others, the fig leaves are harder to identify. They can be patterns of control, or even camouflaged as good works. Good works done to patch a broken identity rather than being the fruit of a Christ-centred identity.

As a pastor for nearly 20 years, I have seen people wear all kinds of fig leaves to cover their broken form.

Are you finding comfort and relief through addiction?

Or maybe like me, you have been pulling yourself together with more acceptable fig leaves.

Perhaps you are in church, but trying to wear the fig leaf of perfection. Trying to be the perfect Christian, the ideal mother, the perfect pastor, the perfect wife, the perfect team member. Again, it is good to strive towards excellence, but not at the expense of your need for a Saviour. Not at the cost of an awareness of your own humanity. Not at the expense of your own heart and your relationship with God.

Maybe you are wearing the fig leaf of control. The only way you know to hold it together is to control the world around you. You have let control become a fig leaf, rather than learning the beautiful and timeless art of surrender.

Perhaps as you are reading this, the Holy Spirit is speaking to you about fig leaves that I haven't even mentioned. False comforts blocking the light, hiding you from a God who loves you.

We begin to taste freedom when we start to understand Christ's love for the woman behind the leaf.

In the words of Tim Keller, '*We are more sinful and flawed in ourselves than we ever dared believe, yet at the very same time we are more loved and accepted in Jesus Christ than we ever dare hoped.*'[11]

And therein lies the place of freedom. Can we come to that place, where the endless pursuit of comfort, covering and hiding, is replaced by a liberating awareness of our own humanity, and an unshakeable knowing that there is a Saviour who covers, who compensates, who fills the gaps? A Saviour who embraces our broken form, and clothes us with His divinity. A Saviour who will energise us to run with His purpose and wear His life. A Saviour who knows us deeply and intimately, yet longs to live on the inside of us.

Freedom is found in our flaws. Freedom is found in knowing love for our broken places, the hidden places, the areas of darkness. Freedom is found in grace, in a wild and reckless love, in abandonment to a love that casts out fear and declares unconditional acceptance.

Can you accept the invitation to the real life?

The invitation to the free life?

The invitation to run with the winds of grace.

This is an invitation to forever be clothed by a Creator who cuts supernatural clothes from His very own heart and wraps them around the sons and daughters of the earth.

Can you allow the one who desperately and passionately loves you to come close, to peel off the layers stuck on from years of trying, and remind you who you are in Him?

To whisper truth and then a more profound truth. To strip off who you are trying to be and to put on who you really are.

I don't know an invitation more beautiful than this. I don't know a wardrobe better. I do not know a lover more passionate and intimate than the One who died for you.

So come, let me take you in to the wardrobe at the foot of the Cross.

THE GREAT EXCHANGE

A Prince was sent from heaven to earth,
To uncover diamonds amid the dirt.
He saw the hearts of humanity dry,
And gave His life to answer their cry.

Daughters created with colour and gold,
Forgot who they were, their clothing sold.
Lost in the lust of earth and its groan,
Naked, exposed, forgotten their throne.

So heaven ripped open to invade her pain,
A rescue planned for the daughter slain.
And on a hill, dark and bare,
This Prince of Rescue drew last breath.

Dressed in the purple robes of a King,
Yielding His life to hear her sing.
A vision alive in an untainted heart,
Forgotten daughters, light in the dark.

Part Three

THE GREAT EXCHANGE

Chapter Thirteen

A LOVE STORY

There are moments where heaven invades earth, and these moments are our very breath, our salvation. Moments when light invades our darkness, and Christ transforms what is ugly to beautiful.

One such moment split eternity. It took place on a cold and lonely hill named Golgotha. The place of the skull, the site where legend has said King David buried the head of Goliath. The place heaven's Saviour, in one last breath, defeated every giant that would assail the human soul.

The Cross on the hill rent open the heavens to declare 'access granted' to the sons and daughters of God.

The Cross on the hill is the ultimate love story.

The place where heaven gave its King for the sons and daughters of God.

The Cross on the hill cries out the passionate love of a Father. It cries out the tender embrace of Christ. It reveals that heaven will stop at nothing to reclaim the place for the sons and daughters of God.

The Cross on the hill will always and forever be the place that we find freedom - the place where transformation moves from a hope to a piercing reality.

The Cross on the hill is the door to a brand-new wardrobe of identity for the sons and daughters of God.

God looked upon humanity and did not see a wardrobe that needed updating, but rather garments so damaged, so stained, so polluted and corrupted, that they were beyond repair.

Our Saviour Himself looked upon humanity and posed the question:

> 'And who would mend worn-out clothing with new fabric? When the new cloth shrinks, it will rip, making the hole worse than before'
> Matthew 9:16 TPT

The sons and daughters of God did not need an update; it was time for a whole new wardrobe.

It was only five days before Christ hung on the Cross that people lined the streets of Jerusalem, acknowledging their King. He rode into Jerusalem announcing to Zion's daughters:

> 'Look, your King arrives! He's coming to you full of gentleness, sitting on a donkey, riding on a donkey's colt'
> Zechariah 9:9 (fulfilled and quoted in Matthew 21:5)

The disciples and the large gathered crowd began what humanity would be doing for decades and centuries to follow:

> They cast off their outer garments to make way for the King of heaven to enter in.
> Matthew 21:6-8

The entry of Christ compels a shedding of the old, to make room for the new.

On Palm Sunday they shed their outer garments to line the streets for the King of Kings. Then every Sunday, and every moment since, humanity receives the same invitation: shed your outer garments and your self-made tunics to make way for the King.

Let Him ride in and take His throne as King of your heart.

In the beginning, the Father slaughtered an animal and made leather clothing for His children, and the outer garments, the self-made coverings - the fig leaves - were shed.

At the Cross, His son, the Lamb of God, was slaughtered. Many say Christ was naked upon the Cross. Perhaps the greatest shame of all for the Saviour of the world. God, stripped naked, so you and I could be clothed.

And in a prophetic picture of heaven's intent, the very clothes they stripped Him of were divided amongst the soldiers; clothing the ones who killed Him.

In a stunning heavenly rewrite, the wardrobe at the foot of the Cross opened up for every son and daughter that would choose to go through the door.

As Christ's forehead was pierced with that crown of thorns, heaven prepared billions of royal crowns for the sons and daughters of God.

A TALE OF TWO CROWNS

For ours was a land
Overtaken with sin and shame,
Until a King came on a donkey
To make His royal claim.

He didn't come as men would think,
Dressed in robes of gold.
Instead, He shed his splendour
So this story could be told.

He rode on streets lined with palms
As people cast their gowns.
He came to claim our inner world,
To restore our crown.

The land he walked was choked in thorns
Until thorns adorned His head.
And for those who yield to His royal claim,
The thorns that choke are dead.

This King, He wore a crown of thorns,
To pay in full the cost,
Of the royal reign of you and I,
Our divine purpose lost.

So now take off your crown of thorns,
Of worry, of sin, of dread.
Shed your outer garments,
As our Saviour's blood was shed.

Strip the cloaks and masks of life,
And come as you are.
This King rides a donkey,
For the gentle, humble heart.

He could have come on a horse of war,
To overtake the land,
But instead, he chose our broken hearts,
As the prize for which he'd stand.

And that is why we trust Him
With our one messy soul,
For dying on the Cross,
He suffered to make us whole.

Chapter Fourteen

THE WARDROBE AT THE FOOT OF THE CROSS

'Now, if anyone is enfolded into Christ, he has become an entirely new creation. All that is related to the old order has vanished. Behold, everything is fresh and new'
2 Corinthians 5:17 TPT

Welcome to the wardrobe at the foot of the Cross.

The foot of the Cross is the only place where I have learnt to change my internal wardrobe.

It's the place where I have understood that what I am wearing on the inside is not a life fashion sentence, but can be continuously changed, reinvigorated, exchanged and replaced.

It's the place where I become aware of the stunning internal wardrobe available for me to put on every day.

At the end of every effort of self-transformation, I find the hand of my Saviour, leading me to the wardrobe at the foot of the Cross.

My attempts at righteousness fail, and my Saviour so tenderly and poignantly declares them to be filthy rags. (Isaiah 64:6)

> And then He takes me by the hand
> and leads me to a wardrobe grand,
> and gestures to a gown,
> purchased by His thorny crown.

This gown is so pure, regal and beautiful, and yet it's so familiar.

It was mine before the creation of the earth. Yet now His blood has paid the price for me to reclaim my robe. Righteousness, untainted purity. Mine to put on. No more striving, no more trying - only a seeing, an awakening, a knowing and a claiming of what is mine, purchased by His blood. Stepping into the wardrobe at the foot of the Cross.

I remember the first time I visited the stunning nation of India - the beautiful, colourful, embattled land that clothes half of our world. It was a gentle entry to an intoxicating nation.

I was shown India through the eyes of one of its beloved daughters - my friend Rachel Waters, affectionately known by me as the Princess Hustler of Mumbai. A daughter who sees the beauty of her nation and the heart of heaven for this land of colour and artistry.

She has a passion for her city that rivals the best, and to see India through her eyes is to see beauty, passion, and artistry at its finest. Knowing my love for fashion, she wove me through many of India's streets until I was drunk with beauty and colour.

In my colour-intoxicated state, she led me into the store of Rohit Bahl, one of India's top designers. I was gone, transported into a heavenly wardrobe. Garments so beautiful, so royal, so colourful and intricate. Created for princesses and wedding days, for brides in robes of many colours. I was lost in the beauty of fabric and design.

I felt the heart of heaven. "Kirrily - imagine what your heavenly wardrobe is like? If these garments can be created on earth, imagine the heavenly clothes I have created for the daughters of God. Kirrily, why would you wear rags, when you can wear royal garments of various shapes, sizes, colours, designs and patterns. Custom made for you. Designed before your birth. Purchased by your Saviour. Found in the wardrobe of His Word. Located at the foot of the Cross for you to put on."

The garments in Rohit Bahl were way beyond my budget. But I knew the garments in my heavenly wardrobe were already paid for in full.

The price was paid by the blood of my Saviour.

And over time I have learnt the currency He requires for us to enter in. A currency He offers every human heart and then invites us to activate to access heaven's resource.

The currency of heaven.

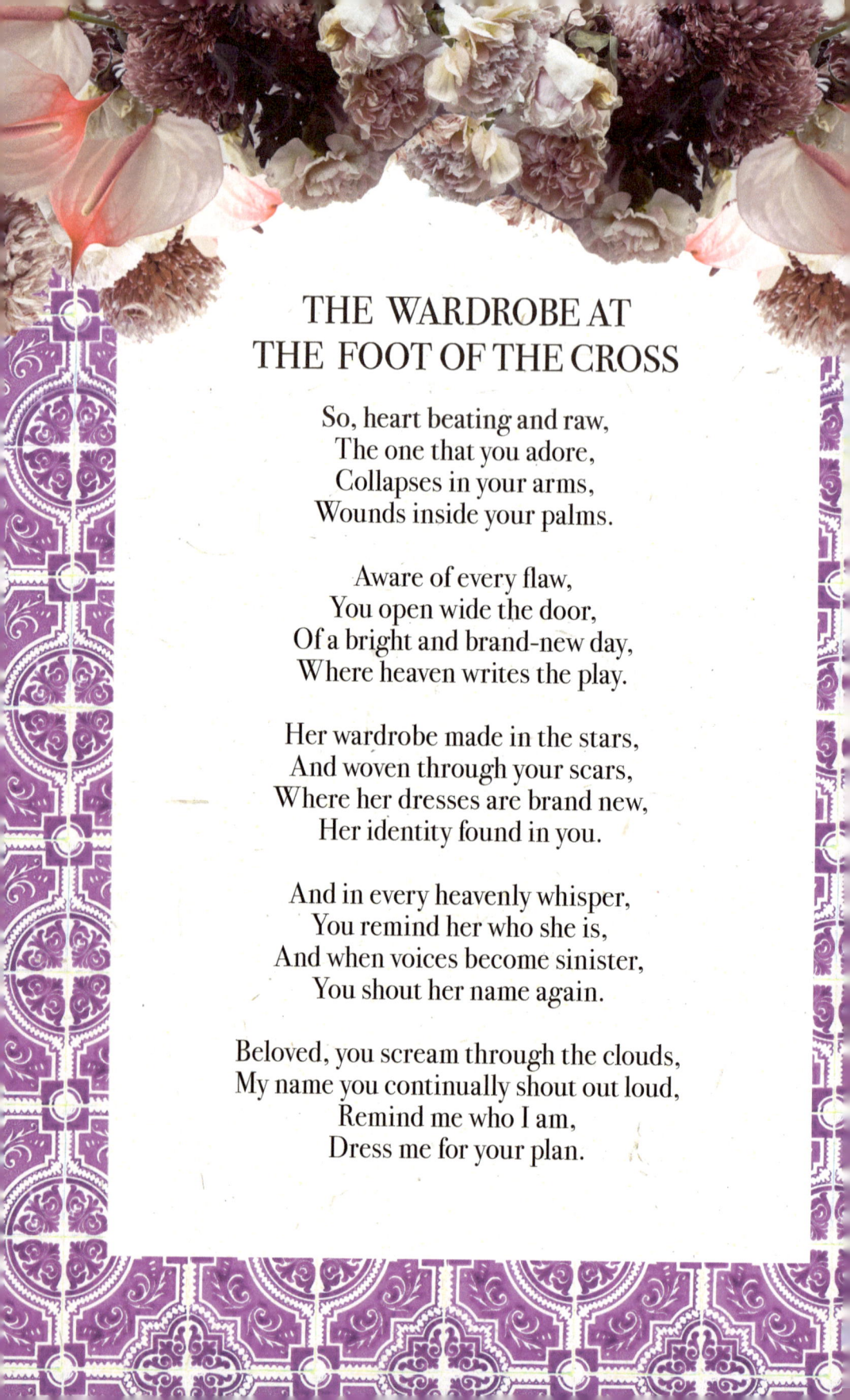

THE WARDROBE AT THE FOOT OF THE CROSS

So, heart beating and raw,
The one that you adore,
Collapses in your arms,
Wounds inside your palms.

Aware of every flaw,
You open wide the door,
Of a bright and brand-new day,
Where heaven writes the play.

Her wardrobe made in the stars,
And woven through your scars,
Where her dresses are brand new,
Her identity found in you.

And in every heavenly whisper,
You remind her who she is,
And when voices become sinister,
You shout her name again.

Beloved, you scream through the clouds,
My name you continually shout out loud,
Remind me who I am,
Dress me for your plan.

Take my tattered clothes,
And dreams now grown old,
And weave them through your scars,
So I can see the stars.

And lead me by my hand,
To the wardrobe where you stand,
So I can be dressed anew,
In a wardrobe made by you.

The woman who I am,
The woman for your plan,
The woman that you adore,
Steps through the heavenly door.

And eyes held by your gaze,
Breathes the air of grace,
And a wardrobe of infinite cost,
The inheritance of the lost.

Becomes her meeting place,
To daily access grace,
To remember who she is,
The princess of a Prince.

Chapter Fifteen

THE CURRENCY OF HEAVEN

I can't buy heavenly garments with dollars, but there is a currency that enables me to access what Christ has purchased for us.

It is a currency introduced by Father Abraham.

A currency for believers. A currency that attracts the attention of heaven. A currency that pleases God. A currency to access that which is in heaven and bring it to earth.

The currency is faith.

I remember hearing the words as a Bible College student. Pastor Phil Pringle boldly declared, 'The currency of heaven is faith.'

And how I've learnt this over the years. There is no getting around it. There is no way to live the bright, wondrous, adventurous life that is yours except by faith. This is how we enter into every promise that has ever been made by the Father. This is how we access the provision of our Saviour, and it is by faith that we claim the heavenly garments of our identity.

> *And without faith, it is impossible to please God, because anyone who comes to him must believe that he exists and that he rewards those who earnestly seek him.'*
> Hebrews 11:6 NIV

> *Our faith in Jesus transfers God's righteousness to us, and he now declares us flawless in His eyes.'*
> Romans 5:1 TPT

Our new creation identity is accessed by faith in Christ, and in all He accomplished on the Cross.

By faith, our old nature, and the tattered wardrobe which plagues us, died on the Cross with Christ. Casting off these outer garments we enter into our royal identity as children of God.

> *Could it be any clearer that our former identity is now and forever deprived of its power?'*
> Romans 6:7 TPT

> *....instead, passionately answer God's call to keep yielding your body to him as one who has now experienced resurrection life!*
> Romans 6:13 TPT

I remember the battle I endured for many years to wear the robe of righteousness.

I remember the years of feeling dirty, unclean, impure and not quite right. Then the moment my eyes were opened afresh to Christ and faith was awakened in my heart.

I remember the feeling of being clothed with the robe of righteousness. The relief, the purity, the sense of wearing my rightful wardrobe.

What I didn't realise is that I would have to fight the fight of faith over and over again to wear this precious robe of right standing with God.

You see life has this way of offering us dirty clothes, of staining our garments, and reminding us who we were without Christ.

I had to activate my faith over and over to access the righteousness that was mine in Christ Jesus.

While I was at Bible College, I would stare long and hard at my new wardrobe, reading over and over in the book of Romans, the provision of His righteousness. It was a daily faith battle, a robe beautiful, blood-stained and hard-won.

Is there a garment in your heavenly wardrobe hanging on the shelf waiting for you to access it by faith?

What is it for you?

Is it righteousness? That beautiful robe that covers the mistakes, the shame, the feeling of being not quite right.

Is it dignity?

Is it honour?

Is it strength?

Is it courage?

What qualities of Christ elude you?

They are yours for the taking.

Stare long and hard in the wardrobe of the Word, discover who Christ is, then apply your **faith** and take those qualities and put them on.

Look, they are a perfect fit.

Chapter Sixteen

THE DAILY EXCHANGE

Just as we need to get dressed every day in the natural, so it is in the spiritual.

Night has a way of disrobing us.

Sleep has a way of messing up our clothes.

I have found that I don't wake every day dressed for success. In fact, I often wake sleepy, half-forgetting who I am.

There are no fashion angels in my household of boys. No fashion angels to wake me up with a rosewater spray, choose clothes from my wardrobe and dress me ready to greet the day.

It is my responsibility to dress myself - to wash off the sleep from the night before and remember who I am. To take off my sleepy throw-togethers and dress ready to meet the world.

It is the same in the spiritual.

When I met Christ, I experienced the radical transformative power of His love, His grace and His acceptance. I thought that I would feel different forever. I thought the mark He made on my identity would be my constant experience. That from that encounter forward, I would always feel accepted, loved, confident, kind, compassionate and full of grace.

But life tears at our clothes, questions our identity, threatens our security and woos us with a culture that is not the culture of heaven.

So many mornings, I wake up having forgotten who I am.

Perhaps I had a dream throwing shame on me from my past. Or the stress of the day before wove anxiety through the fabric of my identity. And I wake not dressed in salvation, not clothed in righteousness, not covered in peace.

It's not that I don't own those garments.

They are there in my spiritual wardrobe, mine to wear. But I need to put them on, they don't automatically float out from my wardrobe to clothe me as I wake. I need to wake up and dress myself.

As babies, our parents clothe us. I suspect that Father God is the same with us. In our spiritual infancy, He sovereignly clothes us with our new-creation identity. As spiritual babies the feeling of transformation is alive as the Holy Spirit attends to the transformation of our spiritual wardrobe.

When I surrendered my life to Christ, I began to feel beautiful as a young woman, as His love, kindness and truth clothed my naked form.

I remember drawing the attention of one young man who didn't know God during this season, and desperately explaining that it was Christ in me that made me attractive. I don't think he was convinced of this, but I was. I knew the difference between me without Jesus, and me with Jesus, and the supernatural beauty His presence had brought into my life.

However, this experience of floating in truth, did not last forever. I had to learn to wake and put on truth.

As I grew as a woman of God, I had to learn to dress myself.

It is a daily exchange.

For me, this looks like waking up, brewing the coffee, sitting up in bed or the lounge, wherever I can find space to myself and opening the Word of God. I may be reading through a particular book of the Bible. I may be drawn to a passage of scripture. Sometimes I am reading a book by another author who understands the wardrobe and wonder of God's Word.

There is always something in my morning devotion that jumps out and helps me to dress for success that day.

Reading the Word is like looking into my wardrobe. But to really do the wardrobe exchange, I need to engage in prayer with God.

I need to come into the presence of God and feel His smile, His love and His acceptance. Then I need to throw off the clothes that are dragging me down and put on the garments that I need to wear to get about the day.

There is rarely a day that I don't have to attend to the state of my wardrobe. I may wake heavy with grief, fear, or rejection.

We can allow those feelings to sit on us, or we can proactively enter the secret place with God and choose to exchange. Sometimes it's an easy exchange, sometimes the process of learning to wear something new can take days, months or years.

There was a season in my life where every day I woke feeling absolutely exhausted and depleted. We had gone through two house moves and a number of years of financial strain. Being a mum of three young boys, an extended vacation was not an option. So, my daily wardrobe exchange looked like me pacing the floor speaking over and over, 'let the weak say I am strong.' (Joel 3:10) It was my way of putting on my garment of strength every morning.

As I write, I recognise my current struggle. To daily strip off the garments of mourning and exchange them for His joy. It sounds simple, and it sounds impossible. But I realise the only way to move out of grief, is to exchange it for joy.

So, each day I choose to become a joy hunter. To hunt for joy in the simple things. In the dawning of a new day. In the sound of kookaburras waking. In the crazy morning routine of coffee, sandwiches, and love. In the voice of friends. The hug of God's presence in the wind and the trees

Love rejoices in the flowering of truth, and I look for the flowering like a hunter sniffs prey. By stripping off mourning, grief and disappointment, my eyes can seek out the truth flowering around me. Then I see the joy of very small things, that speak of a God who glistens with life and hope.

It's a daily exchange.

Chapter Seventeen

CLOTHING ONE ANOTHER

There are times in our life when it is hard to get our wardrobe right all on our own. There are times when we need to clothe each other.

I love to shop with girlfriends, and it is often through the eye of another that we are encouraged to ditch old clothes and embrace something new.

It has been my girlfriends at different times who have helped me to put on spiritual garments I am struggling to wear. They have helped me to put on courage, or at times love, sometimes patience.

I remember when I was new to faith and some older, more mature believers would clothe me over and over again with God's Word. They would dress me in hope, in promise, in love, in acceptance, in grace.

There was my friend, Simone, on a lonely windy beach mid-winter. I felt naked and desperate, and she opened up a book with words that have clothed humanity for thousands of years. Gently and boldly, she offered me the garment of salvation.

Then there was my friend, Felicity, who welcomed me into her home and heart over and over to remind me of my value, beauty, worth and power in Christ.

She was the first to introduce me to the garment of power as she prayed for me to be filled with the power of the Holy Spirit.

I have been clothed over and over again by friends and fellow ministers, in garments of faith, of hope, of courage, of love and grace.

Then as I have grown, I have learnt to dress myself, and have become passionate about clothing other women in the truth of God's Word.

This is really the heart of my ministry to women, a ministry to clothe them in the true garments of their identity as daughters of God.

Every time I stand up to preach God's Word to women, my prayer and hope is that my words clothe them with the truth of who they are in Christ. That the old is stripped away and the new comes forth.

I believe that there is a whole generation of women crying out to be clothed in love, strength, kindness and dignity. As women who have learnt to clothe ourselves, we have a responsibility to clothe others in the beauty and wonder of God's Word.

Imagine us all throwing garments of love over the unlovely and clothing our communities in blankets of kindness, joy and hope.

The wardrobe at the foot of the Cross is abundant.

It is enough to clothe you, to cover your family, your community and the whole of humanity.

Let's dress as many as we can.

Awake, Awake, Put on your strength, O Zion;
Put on your beautiful garments,
O Jerusalem, the holy city;
For the uncircumcised and the unclean
Will no longer come into you.

Shake yourself from the dust, arise,
O captive Jerusalem;
Rid yourself of the chains around your neck,
O Captive Daughter of Zion.

Isaiah 52:1-2

Part Four

PUT ON YOUR
BEAUTIFUL GARMENTS

AWAKE AWAKE

In the book of Isaiah, the prophet cries out to God's people, calling them to awaken and put on their beautiful garments.

As I approach the final stages of writing this book, a pandemic has invaded our world. It is May 2020 and COVID-19 has touched almost every nation of the earth. We are in the midst of a disruption that has not been experienced in my lifetime. In an effort to stop the transmission of the disease, churches have been forced by governments to stop gathering, schools have switched to home-based learning, restaurants and cafes have closed and many businesses shut down.

In many nations, families are required to stay at home, and hospitals are overloaded trying to save the lives of people impacted by this virus.

And the prophets are issuing the same cry as long ago: Awake, awake! It is time for God's people to awake.

Forever, humanity has been plagued with the same struggle. We sleep and we battle to wake up.

We forget who we are and neglect the garments that are ours to put on.

We lay captive in the dust, not realising that we are children of God, with the DNA of the Lion of Judah flowing through our blood.

Though formed from the dust, the breath of the living God lives in us. Yet we often lay captive to the dust and forget to breathe in the air and the life of heaven. We fail to awaken to the winds of the Holy Spirit, and we sleep, dusty and dreary.

We are not called to sleep in the dust. We are called to wake from the grime of everyday life, to shake it off and put on our beautiful garments.

The words of the prophet written thousands of years ago are just as pressing today. And the cry of redemption, freedom, healing and salvation still rings out from heaven to earth.

Life has a way of putting us to sleep. For some, it is the monotony of a life without the oxygen of faith. For others, distress, challenge, trial, trauma and disappointment can exhaust us until all we want to do is sleep.

We want to escape what we are facing, pulled by a culture that numbs us and tries to lull us to sleep.

We switch off our vibrant, believing spirit and close our eyes.

We numb ourselves with TV, alcohol, food, social media, Netflix, pornography, drugs and so on. The list is endless.

As with fig leaves, some of these comforts are not evil in and of themselves. But our choice to depend on them, instead of our heavenly Father, leads us into captivity, where we are ensnared and chained in the dust.

Of course, sleep is essential. It is a gift from God. But slumber is not a state we live in. Rest as God intended prepares us to wake and face the day. Sleeping will not ultimately take us into victory over the challenges in life.

I love the words of my friend Katherine Ruonala:

> I know from experience that it's possible to worship your way out of misery. I've done it many times before. You can become miserable if you choose to just accept your lot in life and try to cope however you can. But no amount of sleep, pleasure, drinking, or distraction is going to get you out of misery. Worship and thanksgiving will. They work. [12]

There is an arising that is called for in God.

It is an arising out of what is natural, what is comfortable, and what seems reasonable.

It is an arising into the incredible woman that you are called to be.

Into the wonder woman found in God's Word.

The prophet Isaiah continued to hear the same thing and issue the same cry.

> *ARISE [from the depression and prostration in which circumstances have kept you — rise to a new life]! Shine (be radiant with the glory of the Lord), for your light has come, and the glory of the Lord has risen upon you! For behold, darkness shall cover the earth, and dense darkness [all] peoples, but the Lord shall arise upon you [O Jerusalem], and His glory shall be seen on you.*
> *Isaiah 60:1-2 AMP*

You see, the prophet didn't call God's people to sleep as darkness covered the earth. He called them to rise.

Rising always occurs in the midst of darkness.

Every rising moment in my life has happened amid troubles and challenges. In moments when darkness has threatened to engulf me.

And every rising has also happened at the beckoning, encouragement and strengthening of God's Word.

It is His Word that is the light in the darkness.

And I am not alone, the great psalmist of Psalm 119 articulates the heart of the risen.

> *Lord, I'm fading away. I'm discouraged and lying in the dust; revive me by your word, just like you promised you would.*
> *Psalm 119:25 TPT*

Yes, rising happens, from the dust, out of darkness, and at God's Word.

I love the vision of the woman of God articulated in Proverbs 31, and her commitment to rise at night.

> *Even in the night season she arises and sets food on the table for hungry ones in her house and for others.*
> *Proverbs 31:15 TPT*

Nearly every significant revelation that God has used in my life to sustain me and to feed others has been born in a time of adversity, in a night season.

I have discovered that if I arise, God is faithful to feed and sustain, and then He arms me with provision for others.[13]

It is hard to dress when we are asleep. It is impossible to wear the wonder of your Christ-given wardrobe when slumbering under the challenges, distractions or even the pleasures of life.

When we wake, we can dress.

Now, if you are a girl like me, who likes to be saved by her Prince, you may be thinking:

'I'll wake up when God gets me out of this mess.'

Or 'I'll step into my destiny when Christ solves my problems.' (Confession: this is a common thought pattern of mine).

Or 'I'll wake up when he wakes up, or she wakes up, or the church wakes up.'

The problem is that these thought patterns are not God's thought patterns. We serve a God who believes in us more than we believe in ourselves. When we cry out to God to wake up, it is not long before you hear His cry right back calling us to wake up.

In Isaiah 51, God's people cry out to God:

> *Awake, God, Awake!*
> *Arm of Yahweh, put on your robe of strength!*
> *Awake and do the works of power as in ancient days,*
> *As in generations passed.*
> *Isaiah 51:9 TPT*

And God replies:

> *I have placed my words in your mouth and have hidden you*
> *in the hollow of my hand to establish the heavens and make the*
> *earth rock solid.*
> *Isaiah 51:16 TPT*

And then again,

> *'Wake Up! Wake Up! Get Up Jerusalem'*
> *Isaiah 51:17 TPT*

As we are trying to wake God up, God is trying to wake us up.

When Christ walked the earth, He did the same thing with His beloved disciples. Caught in a ferocious storm, fearing for their lives, they called for Jesus to wake and save them (Luke 8:22-25).

Then Christ, modelling the pattern of His Father, rebuked the storm, but in the next breath rebuked the disciples for their fear, reminding them to awaken to the faith inside of them.

Once we are awake, we can dress.

Awake to faith, awake to Christ, awake to the authority that you and I have as daughters of God.

Chapter Nineteen

PUT ON YOUR BEAUTIFUL GARMENTS

> *'Put on your strength, O Zion;*
> *Put on your beautiful garments'*
> Isaiah 51:1

For the past twenty years, I have had the joy, the heartache and privilege of pastoring a congregation in the inner city of Sydney.

When our church began, sex workers would take refuge on its steps. Businessmen and women would wander in looking for an inner-city church. Young creatives found a home in a house that preached faith, hope and love.

The beautiful light of Christ was shining right there in the midst of the darkness.

Women from all walks of life have been part of the congregation. The privileged, the underprivileged, the old, the young, the hurting, the healed, the sinner and the saint.

And from the start, I found myself crying out for women to be clothed by their Creator.

That we would put on the beautiful garments that are ours to be worn in Christ.

Before understanding the theology around this message, this cry came from my heart.

Ironically, our church, which gathers in a beautiful old church building, had been used for a time as a fashion house for Tigerlily.

When we took on the lease, we recommissioned this beautiful old church for the worship of God.

But God uses the instruments of the world to preach His gospel, and the language of fashion has become a rich part of the language of our ministry.

Our heart is that the women of Sydney and the daughters of the earth would see and understand their heavenly wardrobe and learn to wear it well.

The contents of this wardrobe are enough to fill a series of books.

In this book, I have focused on fifteen garments that are essential wardrobe items for the woman of God.

Take your time to read through your inheritance as a daughter of God. Each garment is the birthright of a woman who has received Jesus as her Lord and Saviour. It is part of your identity and yours for the taking. You will find that learning to wear this wardrobe will change you, leading you into a life of truth, beauty, victory, authority and love. And it won't just change you once, it will transform you over and over again as you make a daily choice to dress in the wardrobe God picked out for you – clothes designed in heaven.

So open wide your eyes and step with me into the wonder of the wardrobe at the foot of the Cross.

DRESSED IN SALVATION

He has clothed me with the garments of salvation.
Isaiah 61:10

It is impossible to truly experience the life-changing power of God without receiving the gift of salvation. When a woman puts on the gift of salvation in Christ Jesus, all the other garments tend to slip into place.

In my mind, I picture salvation as a glorious wedding dress. But I also like to describe salvation as an undergarment—dare I say, like a spiritual Spanx that makes everything else fit well.

The moment I received the gift of salvation, I no longer felt ugly. I felt like a loved daughter, a beautiful representation of my heavenly Father here on earth. The wardrobe of my identity became a comfortable fit.

I had tried to save myself in so many different ways. The fig leaf of academic success, the fig leaf of career success, the fig leaf of male attention and even the fig leaves of good works. The kind of good works that grow weak without the saving power of God.

I graduated from Sydney University Law School with honours, and still felt empty. I tried romantic relationship after romantic relationship, and again I was deeply unfulfilled.

My idols had failed me, and so I turned to the next thing I knew to do.

I packed up my bags and made my way by bus and train across the wild and long Nullabor of Australia to volunteer at the Western Australian Aboriginal Legal Service.

Surely good works could be my salvation.

I desperately grabbed at doing good like a naked soldier grasping at any item of clothing left on a landscape of destruction and death.

I sought this final fig leaf, failing to understand that good works are only a fruit that grows from a relationship with our God. They are not foliage to cover all that is broken.

In a smoker's carriage, on a train that took two days to cross our nation, I travelled to my final fig leaf.

The memories are blurry, like the carriage I travelled in, filled with the pollution of smoke, and the dying scent of a life of self-salvation that was starting to disintegrate around me.

I made it to that final fig leaf, volunteering at the Western Australian Aboriginal Legal Service. But by then, my wounds were too big and the need for my Saviour too desperate. I didn't last long. The ache inside refused to leave.

It may have only been two weeks, and I was hitching a ride back across the Nullabor with a Swiss backpacker. Still aching for something more. Still empty.

Arriving back in Sydney, I began my six months of preparation to be admitted as a solicitor in New South Wales. I attended the College of Law at St Leonards, where I met a Christian. I hadn't encountered many during my seven years of wilderness living. She preached the gospel, and I passionately took the position of the defence, tearing down her arguments and questioning her Saviour.

But Aslan was on the move, it was my time, and the Lord was hovering like an eagle ready to swoop and claim my heart. [14]

Out of a sincere heart, I asked to attend church with my new Christian friend. It was a little Dutch Reformed Church. I don't remember much of the service, but I do remember deciding to begin to thank God for all that was good in my life.

There was no dramatic encounter, or radical repentance, or supernatural salvation, but there was a girl who had attended church for the first time in seven years and whose heart was starting to open.

That same afternoon I made my way down to North Palm Beach for a swim. It was the middle of winter, the beach was deserted, and maybe I thought that somehow the ice-cold water would wake the spirit of a daughter slumbering in darkness.

The water was cold, but it was the water of God's Word that began to wake me. There were two other people on the beach that day—a surfer and his girlfriend. The bitterness of my emptiness was sharpened against the playful joy of this young couple. The surfer hit the waves, but I encountered the girlfriend as I climbed the sand dunes after my swim. I recognised her as a young girl from the high school I had attended on Sydney's Northern Beaches.

She called out to me, and I was forced out of my covering of darkness and into connection. She asked how I was, and words emerged from my heart that must have by passed my brain.

In one sentence, I answered, 'I feel like I have lost my spirit.'

Within moments she reached for a book. For The Book. The Book that has rewritten the chapters of my life. She reached for a Bible and told me she had recently found all the answers to her life and questions in the pages of this book.

And that eagle hovered over the sun, sand and sea of Palm Beach waiting for this daughter's heart to look up.

How could it be that I had attended church for the first time in seven years that morning, and this same day, on a deserted beach, I would encounter a girl who would open the pages of the Bible to me?

My heart was beginning to open. That evening I went to bed and wrote a simple prayer in the pages of my journal. I didn't realise it was a prayer, it was simply the cry of my heart.

Looking back, it may be the most cringy, cliched prayer ever written.

'Holy Spirit come and live in my heart like a candle that never goes out. Like a candle that keeps burning and stays upright through all the winds and storms of life.'

Then I closed my journal and went to bed.

I will never completely understand exactly what transpired that night. In hindsight, with the benefit of theology under my belt, God worked the miracle of regeneration as I slept.

But to a young adult, all I knew was that the next day I woke to a new world. The colours were brighter, the air crisper, the definition of shapes sharper.

Life made sense to me again. The dark cloud of confusion, despair, hopelessness and emptiness lifted, and I was alive on the inside. Born again, brand new, awakened to God and awakened to faith.

I went to the College of Law that day and passionately began to preach the gospel to anyone willing to listen.

I was a born-again Christian, and for me, the stark difference between darkness and light was too real to ever turn back.

So that evening in my bedroom, without truly understanding my own actions, I reached out and slipped on salvation. I cried out for a Saviour and He answered my prayer.

This poem is my story.

THE GARMENT OF SALVATION

With gentle hands, He reaches down
To lift her from the muddy ground.
A landscape messy, starved of life,
Of dirt and blood, struggle and strife.

With eagle's wings, He swoops her up
From drowning in another's cup.
He sits her right beside His throne
And claims her life now as His own.

The mud He starts to wash away,
As years melt to a bright new day.
Tattered, stained garments are removed,
Every wound is cleansed and soothed.

The broken prepared as a bride,
Breathless wonder at His side.
He brings to her a pure white gown,
And this naked beauty begins to frown.

Then this King, He lifts her face
And all she sees is passionate grace.
She soon forgets about the mess
As she slips on salvation's dress.

In a moment, she is transformed.
The lost and hurting now adorned.
No longer with her face bent down,
This beauty wears salvation's crown.

THE ROBE OF RIGHTEOUSNESS

He has covered me with the robe of righteousness.
Isaiah 61:10

There is a beautiful robe that is referred to throughout the Bible. It is a robe that covers our faults, sins and past mistakes.

It is a robe for royal courts. A gown that dresses us with right-standing before God. It is given freely to every one of us through the gift of Jesus Christ.

Amid the transformation of my soul, I graduated from the College of Law and was admitted as a solicitor to the Supreme Court of New South Wales. I began work as a lawyer, practising largely in the area of criminal law. Before each trial, the barristers would dress in their robes for court, preparing to bring their case to the judge. Clothes for a courtroom. Clothes that gave position and standing.

Just as these robes clothe barristers to bring their case before the judge, the robe of righteousness positions us before God. It dresses us for the courts of the King, to boldly approach the throne of grace, so we can call out for mercy (Hebrews 10:19-22).

Heaven is pure and holy, and we must be clothed in order to enter the courts. There is no sin in heaven. Our impurity keeps us from God's presence. The righteousness that comes from the life of Jesus is our clothing for the courts of a King.

The Lord longs to clothe fallen humanity with His righteousness.

His passion is to cover us with the purest gown.

Like the prodigal son who made his way back to his father covered in sin, shame, and grime, yet his father ran out to meet him with his own robe and ring (Luke 15:11-32).

Just like that earthly father, our heavenly Father runs to robe us in the righteousness of His Son.

For our attempts at righteousness are as filthy rags to God.

> *We are all infected and impure with sin. When we display our righteous deeds, they are nothing but filthy rags.*
> *Like autumn leaves, we wither and fall, And our sins sweep us away like the wind.*
> Isaiah 64:6

It is interesting that the prophet has connected our attempts at righteousness with the flimsiness of autumn leaves. Again, we are taken back to the garden, and reminded of the weak effort of Adam and Eve to clothe themselves in leaves.

The beauty of the Cross pierced our filthy rags of sin and made a new robe. It is His righteousness which now protects our heart as a breastplate (Ephesians 6:14).

And it is His righteousness that gives us a supernatural boldness to approach our heavenly Father and live out His purpose for us. For after all,

> *'the righteous are as bold as a lion'.*
> Proverbs 28:1

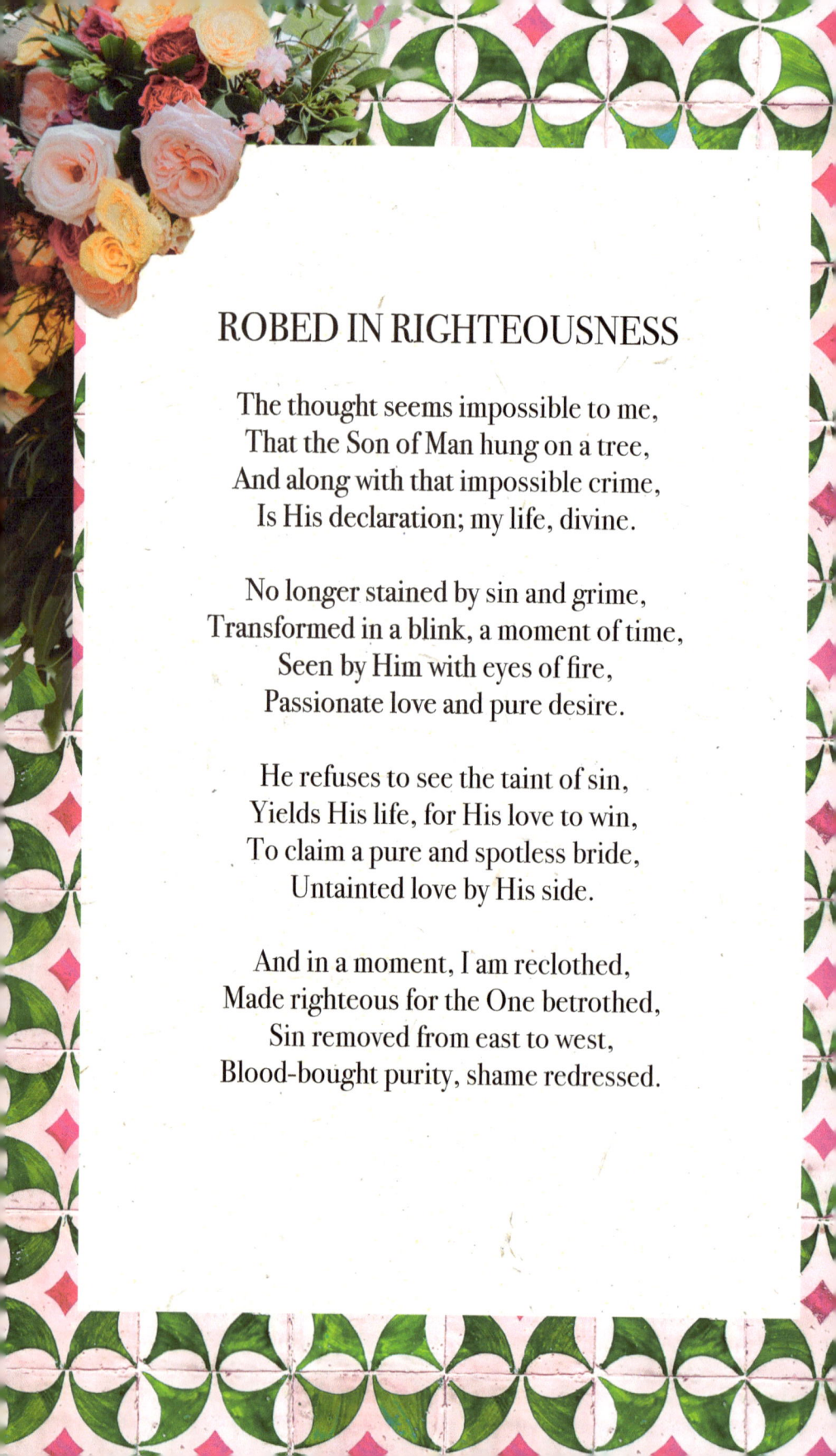

ROBED IN RIGHTEOUSNESS

The thought seems impossible to me,
That the Son of Man hung on a tree,
And along with that impossible crime,
Is His declaration; my life, divine.

No longer stained by sin and grime,
Transformed in a blink, a moment of time,
Seen by Him with eyes of fire,
Passionate love and pure desire.

He refuses to see the taint of sin,
Yields His life, for His love to win,
To claim a pure and spotless bride,
Untainted love by His side.

And in a moment, I am reclothed,
Made righteous for the One betrothed,
Sin removed from east to west,
Blood-bought purity, shame redressed.

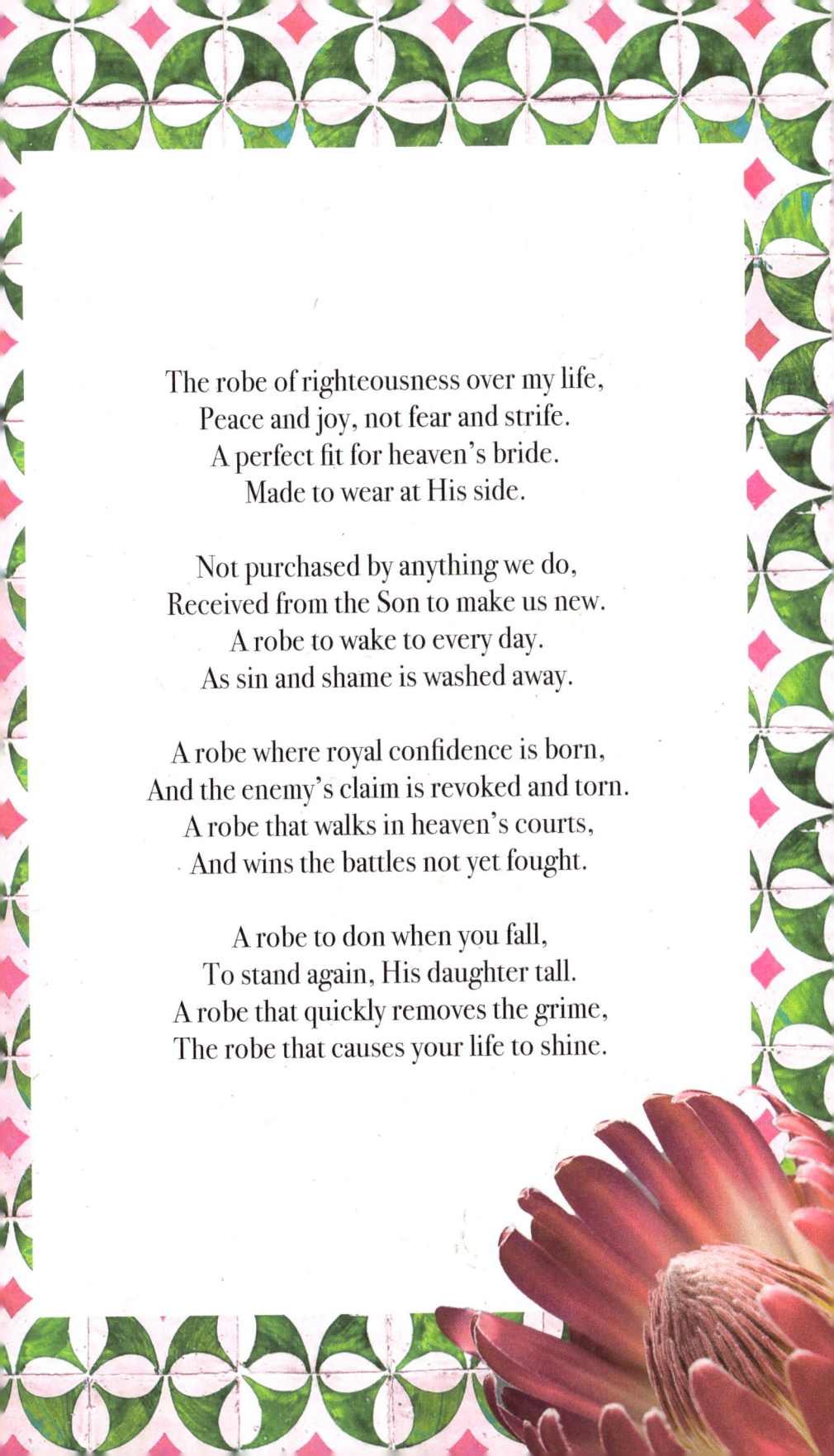

The robe of righteousness over my life,
Peace and joy, not fear and strife.
A perfect fit for heaven's bride.
Made to wear at His side.

Not purchased by anything we do,
Received from the Son to make us new.
A robe to wake to every day.
As sin and shame is washed away.

A robe where royal confidence is born,
And the enemy's claim is revoked and torn.
A robe that walks in heaven's courts,
And wins the battles not yet fought.

A robe to don when you fall,
To stand again, His daughter tall.
A robe that quickly removes the grime,
The robe that causes your life to shine.

CLOTHED IN STRENGTH

Awake, Awake, clothe yourself with strength.
Isaiah 52:1

Throughout the Bible, God tells his people to clothe themselves in strength.

In describing the woman of noble character, King Solomon declares,

'She is clothed with strength and dignity'
Proverbs 31:25

The garment of strength is not for the strong. Christ's strength is for the weak, there to clothe us in our time of need.

Audrey Hepburn beautifully articulated when we need the garment of strength the most. 'I believe in being strong when everything is going wrong.'[15]

As mentioned earlier, there was a season in my life where I would wake up every day, completely exhausted. As a mother of three young children, an extended break was not possible, so in order to put my garment of strength on each morning I would pace the floor and repeat over and over, 'let the weak say I am strong.' [16]

I was far from strong, yet each day I would access Christ's strength to get about the day. Of course, there are days when we are physically exhausted and need to rest.

But I have found that in today's world, so much of our exhaustion is something deeper, an emotional weariness and frailty that the Lord is longing to clothe with His strength and courage.

In the first chapter of the book of Joshua, God spoke to His people three times as they embarked upon their journey to take the Promised Land.

Be strong and of good courage.
Joshua 1:6

Be strong and very courageous.
Joshua 1:7

Be strong, vigorous and very courageous.
Joshua 1:9

There is no doubt that strength and courage is required to inherit the promises God has for our lives. But our human frame so often collapses under the load, and our weakness is exposed. Weakness is not exposed to shame us or stop us, but rather to reveal our need for Christ's strength. In our weakness we are made strong.17

I have found that this garment has been woven on me as I have walked.

In 2015 I wrote the following words:

```
I have worn this garment many times. I have learnt
that it is an essential wardrobe item. I have learnt
there are days, many days, where we will shiver in
the elements without the garment of strength.

I have spoken of the beauty of this garment -
custom made for women of all shapes and sizes, all
personalities and ages.

I have taught women how to wear it, and how to
choose to put it on when every bone is weary from
the journey and the juggle of life with love and
little ones.

I have taught many how to perform the great exchange
- our weakness for His strength - day after day
after day.

Today, I grabbed for my garment of strength, and
```

in the fragility of my own heart, in a season unchartered, I found myself wondering if it was still there — could I still put it on?

You see, I don't want the cold, hardened garment of strength. I don't want the one that shuts us off from the world and blocks out all the beauty and all the pain. I want the heavenly one, the beautiful one, the one full of grace and courage. The transparent one. The tender one.

That's when I felt His hand.

He is weaving this garment upon me as I walk. Woven through the fabric of my heart each day as I get up, look up, and keep walking.

I remember His words whispered to my soul, spoken by a friend and then again straight from His Word.

> 'I will strengthen you and harden you to difficulties, yes I will help you…'
> Isaiah 41:10

This is what our God does. He does not always remove the difficulties, but he strengthens us and hardens us to them as we walk through them.

He tenderly and passionately sews the stunning garment of strength on us as we walk.

One step, one stitch, as strength is shaped upon me.

I am reminded of a quote from my holiday reading — words from Oprah Winfrey, *'I know for sure: your journey begins with a choice to get up, step out, and live fully.'*[18]

My choice; get up, step out, live fully.

The Lord's unshakeable commitment:

To greet us in our getting up.

To clothe us in our stepping out.

To take us by the hand and lead us bravely and boldly into the gift of every new day.

Yes, she is clothed. She is clothed with strength and dignity as she walks with her Creator.

In 2017 I travelled to India to share this message with women. As I was preparing, a beautiful young friend of mine had a vision of a woman standing on an ocean of waves wearing blue. This young one was in her own battle, a battle for life, sanity and voice.

Her vision took place just as a gorgeous young designer named Anjna also travelled to India to work with a master craftsman to begin to create one of the first Invisible She Garments – the Garment of Strength. As this garment of blue and silver was woven, I wrote the following words.

CLOTHED IN STRENGTH

Beautiful, brave, tender and true,
She stands on waves wearing blue.
Clothed not in the strength of a self-made kind,
But in the strength that the broken find.

Woven by threads that form through fire,
Custom made to lift her higher.
To rise through adversity, courageous and strong,
Through the day or years when all seems wrong.

She sets her mind on a bright blue sky,
Refusing to drown in asking 'why?'
As winds are raging and waves beat on,
She wraps herself in the beauty of strong.

With each rising the garment is formed,
Leaving behind clothes that are worn.
Fear, weakness and sorrow fall at her feet,
As she chooses to wake from her sleep.

Mother, sister, daughter, dressed in blue,
Clothed in strength, awake, renew.

Chapter Twenty-Three

DRESSED IN DIGNITY

She is clothed with strength and dignity.
Proverbs 31:25

The dictionary defines dignity as *'the quality or state of being worthy of esteem or respect.'* [19]

Just reading this after a day of children shouting at me, challenges me to dress myself in dignity again before dinner time. Then maybe again before I go to bed, and then again in the morning.

Our lives are priceless, paid for with the blood of heaven's Prince — God's only Son. His piercing threaded a garment of infinite worth, representing our immeasurable value and the unfailing love of God for us.

Life may have stripped you of your dignity. Through abuse, or day-to-day mistreatment in the home, or the workplace. Maybe you have undervalued your own worth, sold yourself to others for a price that is too cheap.

The garment of dignity is still yours to put on. It was provided at the Cross regardless of your choices or the choices of others.

There is an old preacher's illustration that drives home the message of our unchanging value.

The preacher takes a new $50 note. Its value is clear. Then the preacher crushes the note, throws it to the floor and stomps upon it. Mud is smeared on the note. The note is torn.

The preacher then picks up the note and asks if the value has changed. No, it is still valued at $50.

Its value is immutable.

It is unchanging, no matter how it has been treated.

As I write this, I think of women who have been abused. Women mistreated by people entrusted to love them.

I am not sure that there is anything more painful to a woman's soul than to be harmed by someone who God ordained to cherish you.

My heart breaks for this brokenness in the world.

One of the distinctives of Christ's time on earth was the value He placed on women. He saw the unseen, He cherished the rejected, He restored dignity to those not valued. In the words of my friend Mike Connell, Christ came and reversed the false honour system, placing honour on those dishonoured.

I know the feeling of having your sense of worth damaged. Of being so mistreated that you no longer feel good about yourself. I know the feeling of having hateful words spoken over you, of being neglected, and of being rejected.

I know the fight to stand in worth and value when others don't treat you with the value that God has assigned to you.

This is a fight that Christ gave His life for. As He suffered the agony of the Cross, He saw you and me. He saw us bruised and battered. He yielded His life for our redemption. To repurchase us from the hands of the enemy of our souls.

Our value is the value of the King of heaven, the Son of God. It is not based on our performance, or our background, or the words spoken over us. It is based on the life of Jesus Christ.

The daily choice to walk in the value Christ assigns to our lives is the wardrobe of a woman dressed in dignity.

The daily choice to strip off the hateful words of others, the rejections and the piercings of our soul is the daily work of a woman wearing dignity.

It is the Joseph way.

Joseph is famous for his coat of many colours, the mantle of the father's blessing.

Yet, it was early in his story that this very coat of favour attracted the jealousy of his brothers. The coat was stripped from Joseph as he was sold into slavery by those same brothers, and they declared him dead. His coat of many colours dipped in blood as evidence (Genesis 37).

Sound like a familiar story?

Many of us have known the coat of the Father's favour, but life has a way of stripping it from us as we face jealousy, rejection, accusation and betrayal.

The great legacy of Joseph is that he learnt to wear the coat of the Father's favour on the inside, though stripped of it on the outside.

He served as a slave with dignity and integrity. He was imprisoned and still attuned his ear to the needs of others, serving them with the heavenly interpretation of dreams (Genesis 39-41).

Eventually, he was brought up from the dungeon and put in charge of the whole land of Egypt. Ultimately, he was dressed in robes of fine linen and adorned with gold (Genesis 41:42).

Joseph wore dignity on the inside when it was stripped on the outside, and he was positioned to rule and reign as a servant of the Most-High God.

It is the Jesus way. The way of wearing your worth, though others can't see.

It is an exchange that happens yet again at the foot of the Cross, where we daily come to understand our infinite value.

The daily choice to meditate on the unconditional love of God that causes this garment to become a natural fit.

On a flight between cities in India, with the daughters of that nation in mind, I penned these words.

DRESSED IN DIGNITY

Diamonds in the dust of the ground,
Where many say value is never found.
Tried, tested and tempered by the climates of life,
Shaped and clarified through struggle and strife.

Can beauty be found where no-one can see,
When rejection brings us to our knees?
In the places where we are cast aside?
The places where character is refined.

True worth is never tested when the lights are on.
But when the soul awakes to the night song.
Worth unchanging through glory and shame
She wears her garment, just the same.

She knows her value and wears it well.
Dressed in dignity wherever she dwell.
Let rejection and shame fall at her feet.
Diamonds shine as she walks the street.

She picks up others from the dust,
Seeing the value in lives that are crushed.
Her eyes create dignity for others to wear.
She speaks of value, worth and tender care.

The weave of this fabric fills the street,
As women walk to a different beat.
Value established before time began.
Tailors of dignity, reclaim the plan.

THE ADORNMENT OF PEACE

'Let not yours be {merely} external adorning with elaborate interweaving and knotting of hair, the wearing of jewellery and changed of clothes; But let it be the inward adorning and beauty of the hidden person of the heart with the incorruptible and unfading charm of a gentle and peaceful spirit (which is not anxious or wrought up, but) is very precious in the sight of God.'
1 Peter 3:4 AMP

Our world is crying out for this gown.

Anxiety has cast its ugly net over a generation of sons and daughters. Yet the promise of peace stands. The provision of peace through the Cross is complete and irrevocable.

In the words of Isaiah 53:5,

'... the punishment that brought us peace was on him.'

When Christ was pierced with a crown of thorns, He was pierced with every worry and care that has ever plagued humanity.

When we broke the purity of our relationship with our Creator, the Garden of Eden, a garden of peace like no other, became a garden of thorns.

*The ground will sprout thorns and weeds,
you'll get your food the hard way,
Planting and tilling and harvesting,
sweating in the fields from dawn to dusk.*
Genesis 3:18 MSG

When Jesus walked the earth, He warned of the choking effects of thorns. The strangling impact of anxiety.

> *The seed that fell among the thorns represents those who hear God's word, but all too quickly the message is crowded out by the worries of this life and the lure of wealth, so no fruit is produced.*
> Matthew 13:22 NLT

A couple of years ago, I wrestled with worries so piercing they threatened my understanding of who I was, and threatened to rob me of every promise God had spoken into my life. As I battled to throw off my anxiety and move forward into God's purpose for my life, I clearly heard the following words:

'Kirrily, on the other side of anxiety is authority.'

One word can change everything. That weekend, I preached God's word and ministered to hundreds of women.

Many great testimonies came from that weekend. For example, one woman in her forties who had battled anxiety from childhood, discovered a new freedom in Christ.

The Apostle Paul spoke the same words to the young pastor Timothy:

> *'"For God has not given us a spirit of fear, but of power and of love and of a sound mind.'*
> 2 Timothy 1:7 NKJV

Power, love and self-control are on the other side of fear.

Peace is the foundation of power.

Sometimes we have to exchange everything for peace. Surrender every care, every fear, everything we are trying to control. Hand it all over to a sovereign God in exchange for a peace that money cannot buy.

Some years ago, God gave me a funny real-life example of the price of wearing His peace.

It was the end of a gruelling week of moving house.

We landed at Mum's, and the unpacking of our temporary wardrobe began.

I looked for my shoes, ready for Sunday, but no shoes could be found.

I picked up the phone, breathing deeply and trying to keep calm.

'Honey, do you know where my shoes are?'

'Mmm, I remember the bag. They were in a green garbage bag. Are they in the house anywhere?'

'No honey, they don't seem to be anywhere.'

My head was half in the realisation that all the shoes I regularly wore, except the ones on my feet, were loaded in the wrong truck. They were somewhere amid five container loads of furniture and boxes, in storage for an indefinite amount of time. Or the other unthinkable alternative — they were thrown out as a garbage bag.

The other half of my head was thinking about 'The Invisible She Project', and what the shoes of the gospel of peace really mean. You know the scripture:

> '... and having strapped on your feet the gospel of peace in preparation (to face the enemy with firm-footed stability and the readiness produced by the good news)'
> Ephesians 6:15 AMP

I was in a moment of internal conflict. Completely lose it at my husband, or practice what I preach. I made a quick decision and decided to slip on the shoes of the gospel of peace.

Instead of losing it at Tim, I made a joke on Instagram, knowing I would get the compassion and laughter from the girls to cheer me up!

And it got me thinking, we so often think of the shoes of the gospel taking us to far and wide lands. But what about the times we have to slip them on in our own lounge room with our own family?

It seems so easy to slip them on and jump on an aeroplane or jump on stage. It's even not so hard to wear them to a friend's house.

But it's not easy when your husband has thrown thousands of dollars of stunning, on-trend shoes in a garbage truck destined for the tip. And yes, that was the fate of my beautiful shoes. They never did go to storage. They were thrown in the wrong pile and ended up at the tip.

So, on this particular day, my feet were forced to become content in the shoes I was wearing, and more importantly, in the beautiful and becoming shoes of the gospel of peace. The cost was high. It was all my natural shoes. But a price worth paying for the exquisite shoes of the gospel of peace.

The adornment of peace is not something that can be arranged, organised or purchased. Supernatural peace does not come from the world. It does not ensure perfect circumstances, but rather the presence of a person in the circumstances. It comes with a Prince whose name is Peace. It comes from the presence of Jesus.

I spent many years of my life seeking peace by trying to run from trouble and pain. I went looking for tranquillity on the beaches of Byron Bay, the hostels of Europe and the dreamy banks of the Red Sea.

But I have discovered that the peace of God is not a skipping through the tulips, escapist kind of peace. It is a robust peace.

A peace given for the battle, rather than peace from the battle.

A peace that can face giants and take new lands.

A peace that adorns and empowers us to walk on the paths of purpose marked out by our King.

CLOTHED IN PEACE

Beneath her smile, tattered clothes,
Anxious gashes, head, heart, toes.
Not visible to the natural world,
Mind and soul, turmoil swirled.

How do you fix one million breaks?
One million minutes of smile fakes?
How do you push away the fear?
That sucks your breath and draws you near?

Fear transforms into control,
And still, the turmoil has a hold.
She tries to fix the million breaks,
Control the future, no mistakes.

But control carries its own vice,
Vulnerability the sacrifice.
Control, a garment stiff to wear,
Dense, dark, a hooded snare.

Tattered clothes or a heavy cloak,
Both choosing her life to choke.
In the heavens is found another gown,
One million pieces now bow down.

Control and fear yield to trust,
A garment is found, not made of dust.
A gown made from a thousand stars,
From a future seen beyond her scars.

A garment designed from her birth,
Made of fabric, not of this earth.
One million pieces in exchange for this gown,
Peace from heaven, her royal crown.

She wears it on days that don't make sense,
Deep trust and peace, her new defence.
She wears it on the clouded days,
Her gown attracting heavens rays.

It brings a grace from another place,
As peace transforms heart and face.
Consistently worn in highs and lows,
Clothed in peace, her beauty grows.

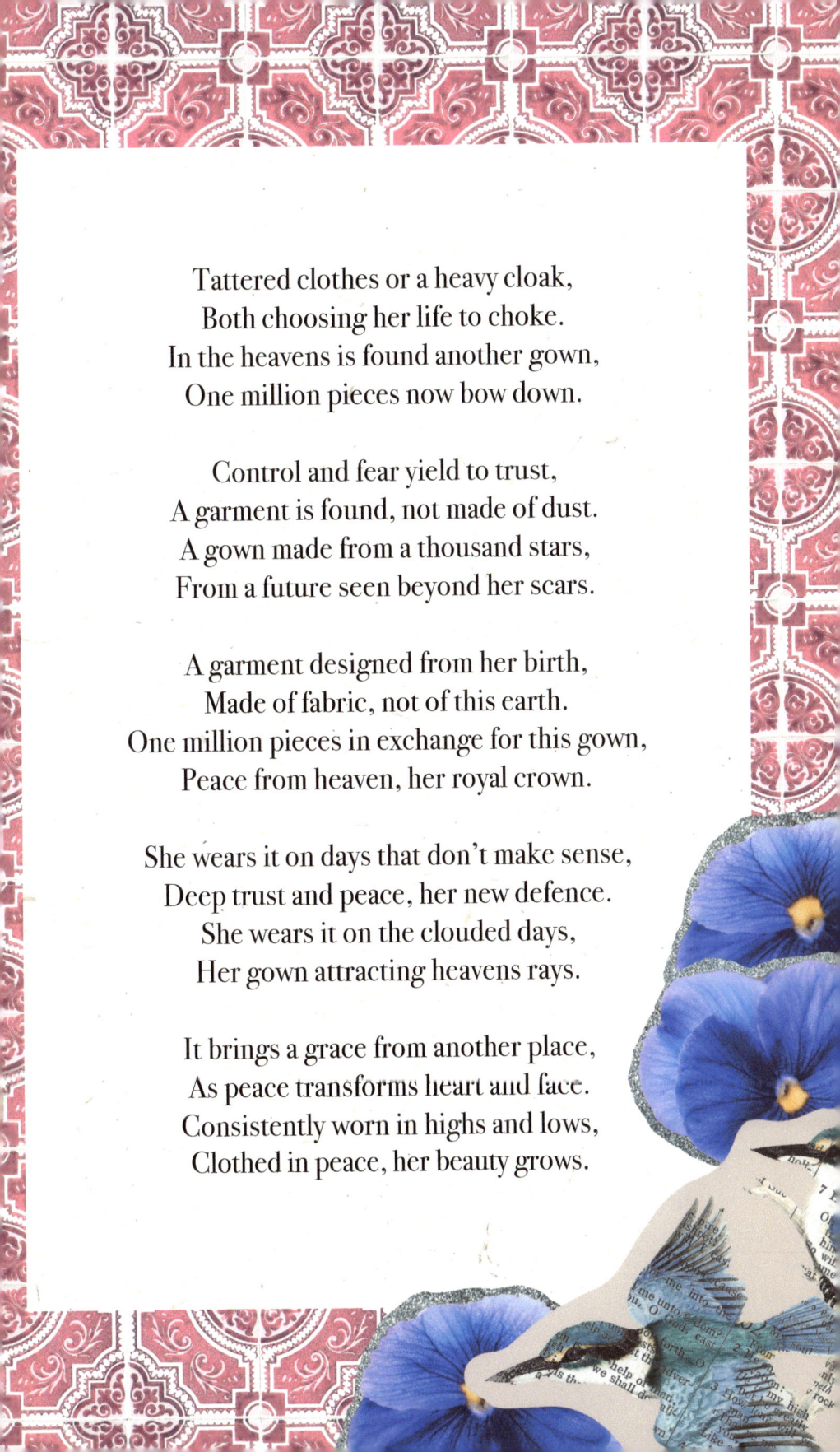

Chapter Twenty-Five

CLOTHED IN JOY

*Then he turned my sorrow into joy!
He took away my clothes of mourning and clothed me with joy.*
Psalm 30:11

One of the greatest gifts of God is the gift of joy. A joy that comes from the Spirit of God living on the inside of us.

I often say that happiness is about what happens to you, but joy is an inside job.

King David found his joy in his relationship with God.

In Psalm 16:11, he writes, *'In your presence is fullness of joy.'*

Joy is a garment that Jesus was clothed with like no other.

In talking of the wonder of our Saviour King, the Psalmist writes:

> *'He has anointed you, more than any other, with His oil of fervent joy'*
> Psalm 45:7

It is the force of joy that sets us apart and strengthens us to get through the challenges of life.

When the Israelites were faced with the daunting task of rebuilding the walls of Jerusalem, their leader, Nehemiah commanded them,

> *'Do not grieve, for the joy of the Lord is your strength'*
> Nehemiah 8:10

It was so tempting for the Israelites to grieve, as Jerusalem became prey to invaders because of the Israelites' own sin.

But Nehemiah knew that if God's people remained clothed in the heavy garments of grief, they would not have the strength to rebuild the walls.

So, he commanded them to not grieve, but to find strength in the joy of the Lord.

Interesting that it was not the joy of circumstances, or what was happening around them, but the joy of Lord.

It is possible to exchange heavy garments of grief, worry and despair for the joy of the Lord. But it is a decision and a conscious choice to make this exchange.

I learnt the power of joy after giving birth to my third child, Elijah. To say that I was exhausted and overwhelmed is an understatement. I was already chasing around after two gorgeous boys, one busy husband and one alive and kicking church. I pushed out my third beautiful boy and went into a four-week battle with recurring mastitis.

Mastitis is the M-word of motherhood. A word I would have preferred to have never been acquainted with. For younger readers, mastitis is a breast infection that is quite common in the early days of breastfeeding. It is excruciatingly painful, makes breastfeeding agony, and comes with fever and flu-like symptoms.

I couldn't see my way through. I was in an ocean over my head, and in this ocean, God started to teach me about the power of joy. The days that I decided to be joyful, relishing in the lovely moments of the season and trusting God each day, I would have the strength and energy to get through the day.

But the days I allowed anxiety, despair and feelings of inadequacy to overwhelm me, I would be drained of energy and lack the strength I needed to get through.

In the most difficult of seasons, I discovered that the joy of the Lord was indeed my strength.

This is a lesson that I have had to continually revisit, and at times needed joy coaches to come alongside me and encourage me in the lifesaving practice of joy.

I will never forget one of the first visits Pastor Ruth Browning made to my home. She arrived on the scene during a time where my reserves were down, and hopelessness was my constant seduction. This time it wasn't mastitis, but several severe relational challenges and conflicts that can come with life in ministry. I was exhausted and fighting despair daily.

She turned up armed with a stunning red lipstick smile, a vibrant Tigerlily cardigan and a mysterious brown paper bag. Ruth pulled a gift of two tambourines out of that bag and announced that we were going to begin to praise, dance and make noise through my house.

It was my job to start praising God with the tambourines.

To practise the art of joy.

I felt slightly awkward. But my respect for Ruth outweighed my discomfort, and I began to shake those tambourines and praise God throughout my house. Then I began to understand that joy is an act of obedience to God's Word.

So many scriptures command us to rejoice. Rejoice is the doing word for joy. The choice to rejoice awakens the joy of the Lord and takes us into a place of strength.

> *Rejoice in the Lord always. I will say it again: Rejoice!*
> Philippians 4:4
>
> *Rejoice always, pray continually, give thanks in all circumstances; for this is God's will for you in Christ Jesus.*
> 1 Thessalonians 5:16-18
>
> *Consider it pure joy, my brothers and sisters, whenever you face trials of many kinds because you know that the testing of your faith produces perseverance.*
> James 1:2-3

How can you begin to rejoice today?

Maybe it's tambourines, maybe singing or perhaps dancing. My personal preference is a noisy private dance party in my bedroom. This simple act of rejoicing has done wonders to shake off heaviness and clothe me with joy.

And for the days where pain is weighing you down beyond your ability to get up and dance, learn the wonder of the Isaiah 53 exchange.

Some griefs and pains are too heavy for the human heart to bear.

So, our Saviour took them for us.

> *Surely He took up our pain and bore our suffering,*
> *yet we considered him punished by God,*
> *stricken by him, afflicted.*
> *But He was pierced for our transgressions,*
> *he was crushed for our iniquities;*
> *the punishment that brought us peace was on Him,*
> *and by His wounds, we are healed.*
> *Isaiah 53:5 TPT*

We give Him our garments of grief and sorrow. And in their place, we take His joy, the joy of the Lord. The joy found in knowing Him.

CLOTHED IN JOY

There is a place where joy resides,
A secret space on mountainsides.
Carved deep in the recesses of our soul,
A force at work to make us whole.

Not dependant on the varied terrain,
A river beneath challenge and pain.
A force that flows from an eternal throne,
That longs to make our heart it's home.

For at night in a field was born a boy,
And angels appeared announcing joy.
In a messy manger, in the humblest place,
Was born a King bringing hope and grace.

The promise of joy for every soul,
Heaven's gift to make us whole.
He came to take the ill-fitting yoke,
Of grief, of despair, the dark, heavy cloak.

And in its place a gown of joy,
The light of heaven from this rescuer boy.
And each day is a choice, what will we wear,
A Gown of Joy or worry, despair?

I bravely remove the dark heavy gown,
And the light of the day smoothes my frown.
I choose to delight in the simplest of fare,
As I wear joy, in exchange for care.

Chapter Twenty-Six

THE GARMENT OF PRAISE

Isaiah 61:3 makes the bold proclamation and promise that our Saviour provides us with a *'garment of praise instead of a spirit of despair.'*

I understand what it is like to wear a spirit of despair.

The Amplified Bible describes this in more detail as a *'heavy, burdened and failing spirit'* (Isaiah 61:3 AMP).

The Hebrew word for despair is *kehah*, meaning dim, dull, colourless and faint.

When hope drains from our being, despair comes to clothe us. Colour seeps away, and the lifeless, colourless garment of despair comes to block our light.

This garment became familiar to me as a child. Patterns in my home life seemed immovable, and as a young girl, the garment of despair became a comfortable fit.

As an adult, when faced with circumstances I was powerless to change, that familiar garment would come and drape itself over my being.

After graduating university, despair had become a familiar garment as I began to realise that my childhood dreams did not carry all the glitz and glamour I imagined.

Being a lawyer was not quite as exciting as I envisioned, and my Hollywood-informed ideals of romance and life were also beginning to shatter.

Life took on a dull shade of grey.

During this season of despair, I made a small and significant decision to start giving thanks for all that was good in my life.

It was within 24 hours of this decision that God revealed Himself to me in an undeniable way that will forever be part of my story. I believe the decision to give thanks took me through the gates of heaven and back into a relationship with God.

Psalm 100:4 teaches us to

'Enter His gates with thanksgiving and His courts with praise.'

I went through the gates of gratitude and into the presence of the King.

Deep down I knew that despair was not a fitting garment for a woman of God. It defied hope, it defied life and defied promise. It certainly was not sparking any joy in my spiritual wardrobe.[20]

I had to learn that even in the darkest of circumstances, there is always hope. In the battle, we can praise, and in every situation, there is something to be thankful for.

I had to learn to wear the garment of praise instead of a spirit of despair.

The garment of praise is beautiful, bright and light-filled. It focuses its attention on the goodness of God and always finds something to be thankful for.

In His presence, praise becomes our gown. For who cannot but praise a God of infinite kindness, power and love?

But in a battle of worship that has raged upon the earth since humankind began, choosing thanksgiving and choosing praise becomes a daily discipline.

I am so thankful for churches that every week begin their services with expressive praise. Some may label this as happy-clappy.

For me, it is the essential discipline of praise that shifts my heart to heaven and shakes off the heavy garments we gather from the day-to-day grit and grime of life.

The garment of praise comes in all sorts of shapes and sizes.

I believe it is custom-made for each one of us.

For some, it is a loud, expressive garment made for dancing. If you have ever visited an African church, you would have experienced this kind of praise.

For others, it is a delicate and gentle garment — a quiet appreciation for all the Lord is and all He has provided. Perhaps this is the praise garment of more contemplative believers, those who practise the quiet disciplines of gratitude and thanksgiving.

It is a garment to be worn in any climate and on any occasion.

I will never forget the story of Corrie ten Boom's choice to give thanks in the Ravensbruck Concentration Camp in Nazi Germany in the 1940s. She speaks of the appalling living quarters of women squeezed together in rat-infested bunkers in the freezing winter. She talks of the Bible studies she and her sister Betsy would run amid these appalling conditions, and of their remarkable decision to thank God for the rats as it kept the Nazi soldiers from interrupting their Bible studies. Their decision to praise in this horrific prison made way for the presence of God to touch women all around them.[21]

David wrote Psalm 7 in a season of travelling through intense accusation and slander. David cries out to God for help, protection and vindication. He ends the Psalm with the following words:

> *But I will give all my thanks to you, Lord,*
> *For you make everything right in the end.*
> *I will sing my highest praise to the God of the Highest Place.*
> Psalm 7:17 TPT

Our highest praise should always be reserved for the God of the Highest Place.

David understood that it was praise that would take him out of the darkness and into the light. After all, it was a prophet who spoke the following words to David while he was literally living in a dark cave.

> *Do not stay in the stronghold. Go into the land of Judah.*
> 1 Samuel 22:5

The name Judah means 'praise'. To move out of our caves of darkness, we always need to move to the land of praise.

As women, may our garments be forever graced with gratitude and alive with praise.

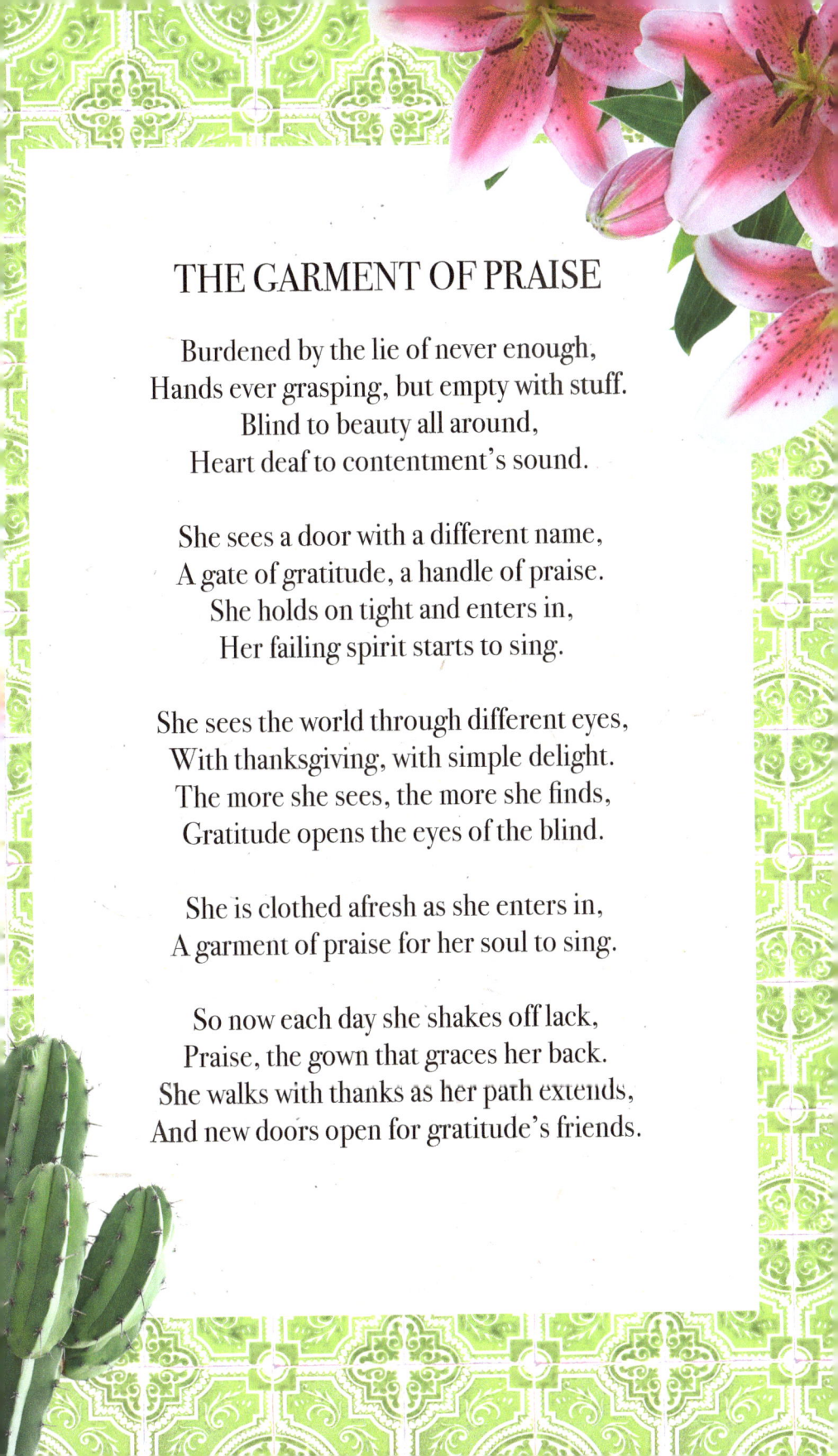

THE GARMENT OF PRAISE

Burdened by the lie of never enough,
Hands ever grasping, but empty with stuff.
Blind to beauty all around,
Heart deaf to contentment's sound.

She sees a door with a different name,
A gate of gratitude, a handle of praise.
She holds on tight and enters in,
Her failing spirit starts to sing.

She sees the world through different eyes,
With thanksgiving, with simple delight.
The more she sees, the more she finds,
Gratitude opens the eyes of the blind.

She is clothed afresh as she enters in,
A garment of praise for her soul to sing.

So now each day she shakes off lack,
Praise, the gown that graces her back.
She walks with thanks as her path extends,
And new doors open for gratitude's friends.

Chapter Twenty-Seven

THE BELT OF TRUTH

Stand firm then, with the belt of truth buckled around your waist, with the breastplate of righteousness in place, and with your feet fitted with the readiness that comes from the gospel of peace.
Ephesians 6:14-15

It is the truth that holds our spiritual clothes together.

It is the belt that keeps everything in place.

I remember taking off my belt of truth and how quickly everything fell apart.

I was a first year Sydney University student, straight out of a Northern Beaches high school. I was young, impressionable and naïve, and my belt was clearly not in place. I thought that universities were the quintessence of truth and higher learning. Little did I know that the classes I took that year would be the very things that unbuckled my belt of truth.

The memory is clear. Sitting in a compulsory first year philosophy class and being taught that all truth is relative. That there is no absolute truth.

In a moment and in a sentence, my belt was undone. I swallowed that lie, and my sense of identity and self started to crumble, along with the simplicity of my faith in Christ.

It was the same lie that was present at the crucifixion of Christ.

When Pilate questioned Christ as to who He was, Christ spoke a sentence that entwined His very being with truth:

> '...the reason I was born and came into the world is to testify to the truth. Everyone on the side of truth listens to me'
> John 18:37

Yet Pilate responded to Christ with the words, 'What is truth?' (John 18.38).

Truth stood in front of Pilate, and Pilate shielded the eyes of His heart and declared 'What is truth?'

True worshippers of God worship in *'Spirit and in truth'* (John 4:24).

Christ came in grace, but also in truth.

Truth holds the beauty of redemption together.

It is fascinating that one loosening of the belt can cause a whole outfit to fall apart.

We are living in an age that bucks the concept of truth. Yet without a firm hold on it, we blow around in every breeze that comes our way. Truth is essential to walking strong through our brave new world.

> *As for you, divinely loved ones, since you are forewarned of these things, be careful that you are not led astray by the error of the lawless and lose your firm grip on the truth.*
> 2 Peter 3:17 TPT

> *This is why it is so crucial that we be all the more engaged and attentive to the truths that we have heard so that we do not drift off course.*
> Hebrews 2:1 TPT

Now is the time for a firm grip on the truth, a time to be attentive to it. It is not the time to be blown by the winds of current culture.

Our belt of truth also comes under threat when accusations fly against us. When all that God has said about us comes under fire.

I wrote this journal entry in 2016 during a personal battle to hold on to the truth of who God says I am.

So, what happens when you are drowning under a lie?

Drowning under people's opinions, drowning under false accusations?

What happens when the stakes move, when the stakes that kept truth secure move, and foundations shake? When the ground starts to move, and your feet begin to sink?

When the battle is hard and long and keeps going, and all you want is for the ground to become secure, and someone to hold up the pillars of truth?

What happens when the only truth that you can rely on is the belt of truth you wear around your belly? When that is all you have keeping your emotions in some sort of semblance of sanity.

Is it time to loosen the belt and let it all hang out?

Or is it time to tighten the belt and walk, head held high through the windy storm of half-truths, lies and false accusations?

It seems that every storm is a war about truth.

Finding the truth and holding onto truth.

I want to be one who tightens my belt. I don't want to be one who loosens it when the storm hits and lets the truth bend or fly out the window.

Windy weather requires secure clothing. We don't step out into a blizzard loosely and casually dressed.

Everything must be tightened, secure and ready for the elements.

And best to secure the clothes before facing the winds. Before standing in the storm.

We need to dress first thing. Sometimes the storm wakes us, and we need to get up, get dressed, and firmly fit the belt of truth.

Secure it before you face the day.

Secure it before you greet the ones you love.

Secure it before you welcome the ones you may be challenged to love.

Buckle it before you meet your accusers. Tighten it before you talk to the accuser in your head.

Wake up, open the book of truth, and then secure all that it says tightly around the core of who you are. Fasten the belt and face the day.

So come, take your beautiful custom-made belt of truth and wrap it around you. It is forged and crafted by the King.

Chapter Twenty-Eight

CLOTHED IN COMPASSION

Therefore, as God's chosen people, holy and dearly loved, clothe yourselves with compassion, kindness, humility, gentleness and patience.
Colossians 3:12

This verse has so much of our wardrobe contained within it. I love how the Message Translation gives expression to this same stunning passage.

'So, chosen by God for this new life of love, dress in the wardrobe God picked out for you: compassion, kindness, humility, quiet strength, discipline. Be even-tempered, content with second place, quick to forgive an offense. Forgive as quickly and completely as the Master forgave you. And regardless of what else you put on, wear love. It's your basic, all-purpose garment. Never be without it.'
Colossians 3:12-14 MSG

Compassion is the first garment listed.

The dictionary definition of compassion is *"a feeling of deep sympathy and sorrow for another who is stricken by misfortune, accompanied by a strong desire to alleviate the suffering."*[22]

Jesus was moved by compassion. It motivated and empowered His ministry.

Interestingly, this very compassion is what compelled Christ to pray for more workers to be sent out into the harvest field.

> *When He saw the crowds, He had compassion on them, because they were harassed and helpless, like sheep without a shepherd.*
> *Then He said to His disciples, "The harvest is plentiful, but the workers are few. Ask the Lord of the harvest, therefore, to send out workers into his harvest field.*
> Matthew 9:36-38

If you have found yourself in a harvest field, it is very likely you are there as a result of Christ's prayer.

And now, it's our turn to clothe ourselves with compassion and represent our Saviour.

Almost sixty years ago in the soil of a war-torn heart, a young minister learnt how to exchange hatred for compassion and went on to lead the first Marist Brothers Mission to Japan.

That young padre was my Great Uncle Lionel, and his legacy is imprinted upon my heart.

On 15 February 1942, Uncle Lionel was captured by the Japanese in Singapore, along with other Australian soldiers. History speaks of the slave labour on the Burma-Thai railroad at the hands of the Japanese during this period of captivity, the inhumane treatment of the prisoners of war and their shocking death rate.

Uncle Lionel was serving as a military chaplain during this time. During his capture, the military padre was allowed to move among his fellow Australians working on the railroad, visiting those dying, burying the dead and occasionally organising Mass.

On one occasion, Uncle Lionel was walking along the rail track when he saw a Japanese officer hitting several emaciated prisoners with his swagger stick, for no apparent reason. As a man of justice, clearly related to me, Uncle Lionel moved up, saluted and said to the officer, 'Sir, I protest. Your actions are against the Geneva Convention rules for prisoners of war.'

Unfortunately, this civilised attempt at justice failed, and the officer grabbed my half-starved great uncle, spun him around and kicked him down the steep embankment.

It is said of my uncle that 'murderous anger surged through his brain, sweeping aside all constraints against hating.' From that point on, Uncle Lionel's mood began to change—from hatred to a bleak feeling of hopelessness and depression.

This darkness eventually drove my Uncle Lionel to his knees where he asked God's forgiveness for hating and promised the Lord that should he survive the war, he would go to Japan to preach the gospel of love.

Over the next few days, the peace in my great uncle's heart returned, and the darkness and depression lifted. Uncle Lionel stripped off the heavy ill-fitting garment of hatred and put on forgiveness, love and compassion.

Upon his return to Australia, he stunned many with his attitude to the Japanese. He did not equate the Japanese people with the sadistic POW (Prisoner Of War) guards. Instead, he saw the guards as a product of brutal military training methods. Father Paul Glynn recounts, 'He seemed to be the only public voice we heard in Australia that expressed positive, helpful ideas about the Japanese.' [23]

In May 1949, Uncle Lionel landed on Japanese soil to preach the gospel.

He was clothed in compassion, he was moved by compassion, and he founded the first Marist Brothers Mission to Japan.

No matter what the state of your heart is currently, at the foot of the Cross, Christ can change the ugliest garments into garments of beauty that will transform our world.

Yes, the garment of compassion came at a cost for my great uncle. It cost him hatred, bitterness and his own desire for revenge. It cost him humility and sincere repentance. But no doubt this garment has reaped an eternal reward in the lives of those who experienced his forgiveness and grace.

Yes, compassion comes at a cost.

But compassion carries power.

When Christ was moved with compassion, He raised the dead, healed the sick, fed the hungry, restored sight to the blind and forgave sin.

Compassion is a conduit for power and is part of our new creation identity.

It's who we are as women of God.

> Let us not become weary in doing good, for at the proper time we will reap a harvest if we do not give up.
> Galatians 6:9

Each waking day we can strip off weariness and compassion fatigue, and clothe ourselves afresh with the compassion of Christ.

It may cost time, money and energy, but this garment will bring heaven to earth.

Chapter Twenty-Nine

CLOTHED IN KINDNESS

Therefore, as God's chosen people, holy and dearly loved, clothe yourselves with compassion, kindness, humility, gentleness and patience.
Colossians 3:12

She opens her mouth with wisdom and on her tongue is the law of kindness.
Proverbs 31:26

Kindness is an everyday virtue, a wardrobe staple for a woman of God.

The Hebrew word for kindness is *chesed*, and the Greek word is *chrestotes*. Both words convey emotion and action. Kindness is love in action, one of the doing words for love.

Kindness has the power to disarm the hardest heart, to change the course of someone's future, and I believe ultimately to change a city.

Kindness has the power to turn people to God, and the lack of it can turn people away from God.

> *Kindness from a friend should be shown to a man without hope, or he might turn away from the fear of the All-powerful.*
> *Job 6:14 NLV*

Kindness has the power to break through anxiety and depression — two of the most crippling forces in our generation.

> *Anxiety in the heart of a man causes depression, but a kind word makes it glad.*
> *Proverbs 12:25 NKJV*

Kindness is a natural fit for a woman of God. It dresses our thoughts, our mouth and our actions.

I remember returning from a mission's trip to Uganda.

I was tender from exposure to so much heartache and pain, a little raw from culture shock and exhausted from two weeks of very little sleep. Throughout the trip, I did my very best to show the kindness and love of God to all I encountered. I had the privilege of meeting my Compassion Sponsor Child, Solomon, and show kindness to his family as they recovered from civil war and extreme poverty. I was filled with joy as I gave out to others. However, upon my return, I was depleted as I struggled to process the pain and poverty of another nation.

As I landed back in Sydney, the Holy Spirit spoke to me clearly, "Kirrily, be kind to yourself."

I realised that to replenish my own soul, I needed to be gentle and kind to myself. I sense that this may be a word for other women reading. To consistently wear the kindness of God to the world around us, we need to receive God's kindness ourselves.

It is challenging to wear kindness if we haven't learnt to accept God's tender kindness toward ourselves.

Then we must learn to wear it at home with our family. This is often where we need it most of all. Daily stress and strain can rip and pull apart our garment. We need to visit our heavenly wardrobe often, calling upon the kindness available to us in Christ Jesus.

In 2016 I released the fifth book in The Invisible Tree Series, Kindness.[24] It was Mother's Day, and we planned to launch the book in our Sunday Service as a celebration of the kindness of mums. I was preaching and reading the book publicly for the first time. My mum was coming to church as well as all the kids, of course. I rushed around, getting ready for the service.

Each book in The Invisible Tree Series has a natural fruit representing one of the fruits of the Spirit.

In Kindness, the kindness fruit is represented by a pineapple.

In our foyer at home, we had a beautiful golden ceramic pineapple. I decided to take the golden pineapple to church to help with my message. After unwrapping gifts from the kids, I ran upstairs to quickly shower.

In the shower, as I ran through my message on 'Kindness' in my head, I heard an almighty crash.

As I emerged from the bathroom, one of my boys (not to be named) ran up the stairs to let me know that they had broken the coconut!

I took a deep breath and questioned them about which coconut they were referring to, as I didn't recall having one in the home. He replied, 'you know, Mum, the golden one'. I took a moment, and I am proud to say I kept on my garment of kindness, told my little boy that it was OK, and took my beautiful golden pineapple to church in broken pieces.

The golden pineapple was broken, but everyone's heart was intact, and it was a beautiful morning. My broken pineapple made a great sermon illustration, and a week later, a legend in our church presented me with a beautifully repaired pineapple.

So, here are the words from the Kindness book.

I pray they speak to your heart.

KINDNESS

Someone once told me about a word,
A word so lovely it must be heard.
A word that makes music in the street,
A word that wakes very tired feet.

If only I could catch this sound,
I could turn the world around.
Like streams of water in a dry land,
Is the word of kindness in my hand.

If I catch it, must I give it away?
For I really want this word to stay.
But this word has dancing feet,
It jumps on everyone I meet.

The only way this gift will stay,
Is if I let it have its way!
It wants to change the way I think,
When my thoughts begin to sink.

After my thoughts, it gets in my mouth,
And turns my words north from south.
When I want to say something cruel,
It reminds me of the golden rule.

Would I like it said to me?
Of course not, so I count to three.
And instead I say something kind,
And I like the smiles that I find.

Kindness will change what I do,
Now I include my brother too.
I pick a flower when he is sad,
And help out my mum and dad.

I love this word and I like it's sound.
I need to know where is it found.
I looked everywhere, but I couldn't see,
Until I looked on the inside of me.

And there it was, it was inside,
It's a fruit that does not hide.
This word's not such a mystery,
It's alive on my invisible tree.

Chapter Thirty

THE GARMENT OF HUMILITY

Therefore, as God's chosen people, holy and dearly loved, clothe yourselves with compassion, kindness, humility, gentleness and patience.
Colossians 3:12

True beauty is found not in the spotlight, but in the place of humility.

Humility is not having a poor opinion of ourselves. But instead, aligning our sense of worth with the infinite value God places on us, and in the process emptying ourselves of the need to prove it to others.

False humility will stop us from going through God-given doors. False humility makes us less than the person that God created us to be, and will rob us of the confidence to seize the opportunities God places in front of us. Sometimes rejection will dress itself up as false humility and limit the path ahead of us.

Genuine humility will journey through doors of gold and doors of nails, and make it through to the other side.

While negotiating some tough doors in 2016, I wrote the following:

There are some doors we are called to travel through that demand specific clothing.

Our everyday clothing won't cut it. Our humanity won't cut it. Our own strength won't cut it, heavenly clothes are called for.

These are the passages of old, traversed by the saints, old and new.

Passageways that will rip our earthly garments to shreds until we look up and see a new wardrobe, heavenly garments, available for us to put on.

Some doors just won't open until we change our clothes. We need our eyes to be healed to see the garment required.

There are passageways where arrows fly, and we grope in the dark—our path blocked until the light is turned on and we can see.

There are passageways where our identity is under fierce attack. Where our heart is pierced, and fiery darts drive their sharp tips through our soul.

While on earth, Jesus never graduated from this piercing attack.

From the humble birth in the manger, to the testing in the wilderness, which began with, *'If you are the Son of God.'*[26] Then to His last moments on the Cross, taunted by the same brutal attack;
'If you are the Christ, come down from the cross.'[27]

While He was housed in a body of flesh, the attack on Jesus' identity was relentless. And I am starting to realise that on this earth, this may not be an attack we ever graduate from either.

So how do we travel the passageways where the arrows are flying? How do we get to our destination, with fiery darts seeking to pierce our heart?

Jesus used an unusual garment to travel the passageways where His identity was under attack. I am starting to recognise it as the garment of humility. He did not assert His divinity; He gave it up for service.

His choice and responses wove a new heavenly garment for us, a garment articulated in all its beauty in Philippians 2.

> *Have this same attitude in yourselves which was in Christ Jesus [look to Him as your example in selfless humility], who, although He existed in the form and unchanging essence of God [as One with Him, possessing the fullness of all the divine attributes—the entire nature of deity], did not regard equality with God a thing to be grasped or asserted [as if He did not already possess it, or was afraid of losing it]; but emptied Himself [without renouncing or diminishing His deity, but only temporarily giving up the outward expression of divine equality and His rightful dignity] by assuming the form of a bond-servant, and being made in the likeness of men [He became completely human but was without sin, being fully God and fully man].*
> *Philippians 2:5-7 AMP*

He wore humility.

He did not need to grasp at His identity, defend His identity or assert His identity, because He knew His identity. He wore humility and made way for us through a narrow passage where darts are aplenty.

He kept on His breastplate of righteousness. He held firm His shield of faith, and He held tight to the garment of humility. Holding it close when others fiercely demanded He take it off and put on His royal robes.

I guess they didn't realise, He was already wearing His royal robes. Humility is the garment of kingdom royalty.

Humility is the cloak that covers you in passageways of dishonour and brings you into the throne of the King.

Humility hides us, protects us, covers us, and brings us into the kinship of God's Son.

It is beautiful and available for you to put on.

Rest in your identity as a much-loved child of the King and clothe yourself in humility today.

Chapter Thirty-One

GRACED WITH GENTLENESS

Therefore, as God's chosen people, holy and dearly loved, clothe yourselves with compassion, kindness, humility, gentleness and patience.
Colossians 3:12

...cultivate inner beauty, the gentle, gracious kind that God delights in.
1 Peter 3:4 MSG

It was 2015, and my husband and I were sitting at a pastor's conference. Amid training, teaching, laughter and meals came a word that cut through the how-tos of ministry and pierced my soul.

My friend, Martyn Webb, Senior Pastor of C3 Spectrum, Nelson Bay, was asked to prophesy over the group.

Marty began to prophesy about a new garment of gentleness that would clothe God's people to enable us to reach a hurting and broken world. The words were like water to my war-weary soul.

Gentleness felt like a birthright to me as a daughter of God. But, in the battles of life, this timeless gown, this fruit of God's Spirit seemed lost and dusty in the back of the cupboard, trampled by wartime garments of strength, courage, boldness and faith.

I found it hard to grapple with the concept of wearing gentleness in my household of assertive men. The garment didn't seem to cut it in many of the ministry battles I found myself in. A garment that was once a natural fit seemed too delicate for the life the Lord had given me.

So, this word from Marty entered deep into my spirit, as a word I knew to be true but didn't know how to apply in the rough and tumble of life.

Fast forward five years, it is 2020, and the winds of adversity and a global pandemic lead me to my knees. Sometimes the only way to make it through hardship is on our knees. I draw close to my Saviour, in deep dependence on His presence.

And I hear the words:

> *Come to me, all you who are weary and burdened, and I will give you rest. Take my yoke upon you and learn from me, for I am gentle and humble in heart, and you will find rest for your souls. For my yoke is easy and my burden is light.*
> *Matthew 11:28-30*

I realise there are burdens we carry that shift in the presence of gentleness. Gentleness of spirit eases the weight of a weary world. I realise there are weights I wear because I have failed to wear the gentleness found in my heavenly wardrobe.

Jesus yearns to remove our burdens by teaching us to live like Him, to walk with a gentle and humble heart. These virtues are a beautiful fit for our tired souls, replacing the weights of self-effort with the grace of a gentle and humble God.

It is with hands of gentleness that God touches the hearts of hurting people. And it is with hands of gentleness that God calls His people to minister to a hurting world.

Gentleness is a garment that gives us access to hard hearts and impossible circumstances.

The Jesus warrior wears gentleness with victory and strength.

I love the poignant words of Erwin McManus in his book The Way of the Warrior, when he says that, '**The warrior is not ready for battle until they have come to know peace.**' [28]

This speaks to me of the quest to wear gentleness in battle. When we master internal peace amid war, gentleness becomes a natural fit.

Christ modelled this garment in His surrender to the Father amid brutality, accusation and violence. As McManus notes:

"The cross will be forever remembered, long after time ceases to exist, not just as a declaration of the one who stands victorious but as a promise that in the end war will surrender to peace. It is the way of Jesus that is the ancient path to inner peace. His life is the way of the warrior."[29]

The Apostle Paul learnt to put on gentleness in a prison cell, penning these words from a Philippian prison:

'Let your gentleness be evident to all ... the Lord is at hand'
Philippians 4:5 NKJV

And I believe that is the key to wearing gentleness in every circumstance; knowing that the Lord is closer than our very breath. The Lord is at hand. When we want to scream, we can choose gentleness instead, for He is right here with us.

Hebrews 12 gives us similar encouragement about how to run the race of our life with passion and determination amid the wounding that comes from others and the sin that comes from our own fallen nature.

We look away from the natural realm and fasten our gaze onto Jesus who birthed faith within us and who leads us forward into faith's perfection. His example is this: Because his heart was focused on the joy of knowing you would be His, He endured the agony of the Cross and conquered its humiliation, and now sits exalted at the right hand of the throne of God!
So consider carefully how Jesus faced such intense opposition from sinners who opposed their own souls, so that you won't become worn down and cave in under life's pressures. After all, you have not yet reached the point of sweating blood in your opposition to sin.
Hebrews 12:2-4 TPT

Jesus points the way. He was sweating blood and yet wore gentleness. He forgave and yielded His life to the Father.

He is our example, and His gentleness our gown.

Chapter Thirty-Two

CLOTHED IN PATIENCE

'Therefore, as God's chosen people, holy and dearly loved, clothe yourselves with compassion, kindness, humility, gentleness and patience. Bear with each other and forgive one another if any of you has a grievance against someone. Forgive as the Lord forgave you. And over all these virtues put on love, which binds them all together in perfect unity.'
Colossians 3:12-14

The Cambridge Dictionary defines patience as *'the ability to wait, or to continue doing something despite difficulties, or to suffer without complaining or becoming annoyed.'* [30]

Even as I read this definition, I realise my garment of patience needs desperate attention.

The Biblical definition of the word is closely linked to the word longsuffering, and I am not surprised!

For a long time, I defined patience as that ugly green jumper that I never wanted to wear. Until of course, I discovered it was absolutely necessary when the weather turned cold. The winter. The times of waiting. The times where the flowers failed to bloom and the leaves on the trees wither.

I have battled with this garment like a child who will not allow her parents to dress her.

In 2014 I penned these words:

There are seasons in life where your clothes need to change. Where, to survive the cold, the wind, the rain, the harsh climate, you need to rug up in clothing that will see you through.

There are winter seasons. They are cold and hard to understand. Devoid of flourishing life. Painful, painfully cold.

In winter, you feel like sleeping. Hibernating just to get through.

I cry out to God, I don't feel made for the winter. Surely, I am designed for the flourishing fun of summer. For cocktail dresses and beautiful sunsets. For long bright days, and endless laughter.

Winter hurts.

I look for the fruit, and there is none. I look for the flourishing trees, and they are bare.

I long to run with bare shoulders; free, warm, light. Yet every day I wake and have to keep putting on clothes, more clothes, His clothes.

Yes, He created the seasons, my master and my Lord.

This little tree is screaming. Give me summer. Cause me to flourish.

I am stripped bare. The fruit is gone, the leaves are falling.

Can my heart endure the winter without being frozen through?

The heart must remain through winter. It must learn and rest and grow through winter. Winter was not designed to kill the tree but to allow the tree to rest, to recover, for the roots to go deeper.

Winter is not designed to destroy; it is preparation to deploy.

But winter requires something different from me. When it seems like we are going without, it is the season to work within.

I begin to study trees in winter.

There are dangers.

The bark can freeze. The tree can be damaged.

What to do when you feel like you are freezing through?

Sometimes they clothe trees, they clothe the bark to stop it from freezing.

And I know I need to be clothed. I know I need to dress for winter.

There are winter clothes. Clothes like patience, endurance and hope.

As a child, I rejected the warmth of winter clothes. But now I am an adult, and my parents can't force clothes on me. I must use my maturity and choose to wear the winter garments. Choose to wear the beauty of patience till spring begins to blossom.

So, Lord, help me to strip off my weak, broken and ill-fitting garments of impatience and selfish demands and help me to clothe myself in the beauty of winter.

For each season is ordained by you. Each season has its purpose. Each season has its garments.

Patience is needed for the life of the long-distance run, the endurance event, the pilgrim's journey.

I hear His words;

> 'You need the strength of endurance to reveal the poetry of My will and then you will receive the promise in full.'
> Hebrews 10:36 TPT

The garment of patience is not an optional extra.

To see His poetry, this garment is essential. It keeps us in His story. Makes us part of His story.

I lift my arms, and He slips it on. The beautiful, robust and costly garment of patience.

And I am reminded of the words I wrote to children articulating our journey of growing in patience, and I know they are words for grown-ups too...[31]

PATIENCE

I waited and waited patiently,
For something I wanted desperately.
I asked once and I asked twice,
I even tried to be really nice.

But when after a while it didn't come,
I stomped my feet and said, "I am done."
I was tired of waiting so long,
My waiting heart was not so strong.

And still, and still it didn't come!
But, I knew I really wasn't done.
I would wait and wait and wait,
To see that postman at the gate.

For that thing was surely on its way,
Planned for a very special day.

I wanted that postman to find me there,
Not given up in despair!
And He would say gently,
"Well done, for waiting patiently."

Then I opened my surprise,
And that thing appeared before my eyes!
But more surprising than that thing,
Was something the postman didn't bring.

Something I found down deep inside,
A fruit called Patience come alive.
And this fruit was not a boring thing,
This patient fruit did help me sing!

My thoughts about Patience were wrong,
This is a fruit that makes you strong.

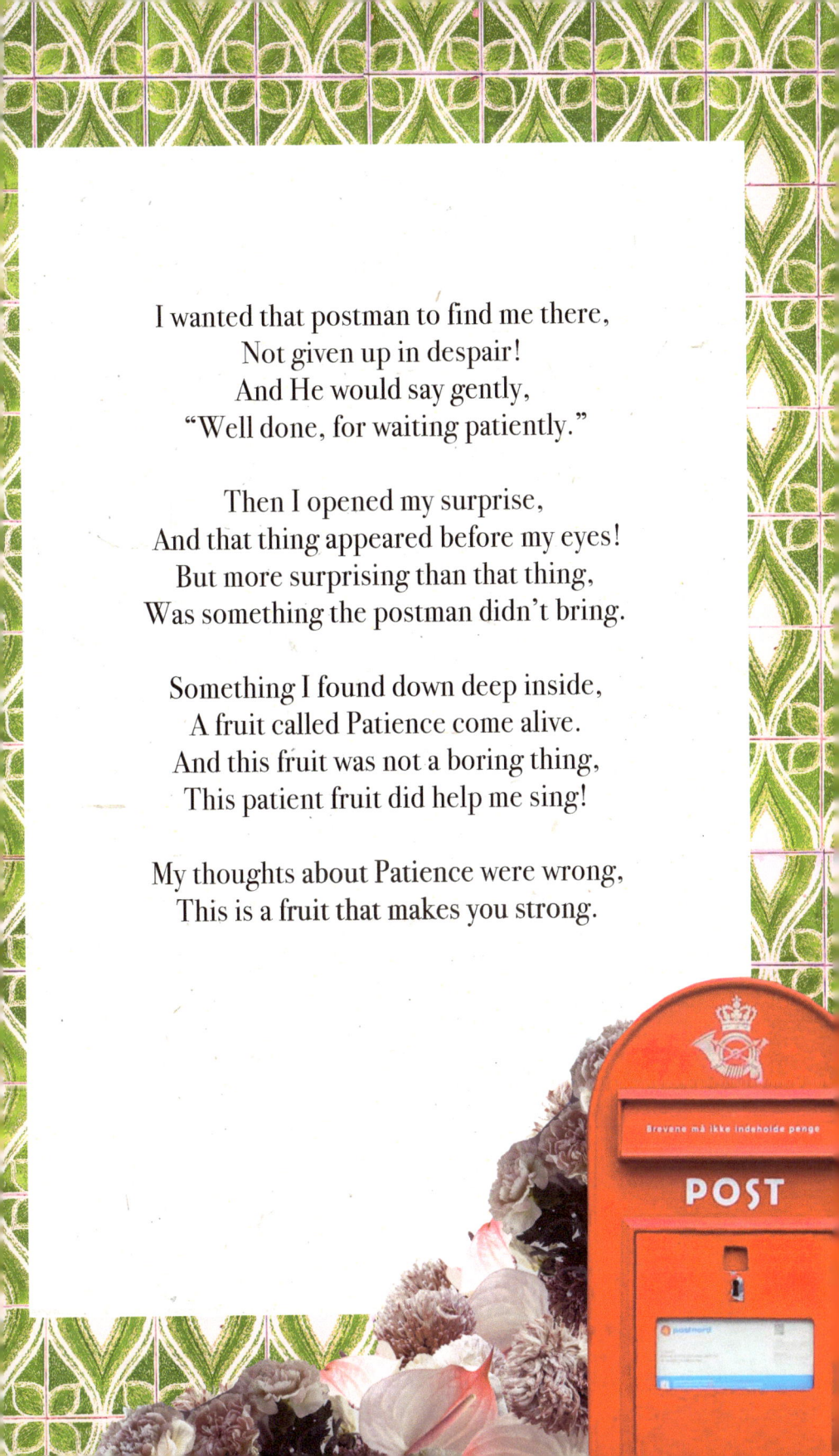

LAYERS OF LOVE

And over all these virtues put on love, which binds them all together in perfect unity.
Colossians 3:14

Love is the garment above all the others. The garment that binds everything else together in perfect unity.

The Apostle Peter came to the same conclusion as the Apostle Paul.

> 'Above all, love each other deeply, because love covers over a multitude of sins'
> 1 Peter 4:8

A coverall garment that covers a multitude of sins.

A garment that fulfils all the commandments.

A garment that covers flaws in the unconditional love of God.

> *Teacher, which is the greatest commandment in the Law?*
> *Jesus replied: "Love the Lord your God with all your heart and with all your soul and with all your mind. This is the first and greatest commandment.*
> *And the second is like it: Love your neighbour as yourself.*
> *All the Law and all the Prophets hang on these two commandments."*
> Matthew 22:36-40

This question was asked of Christ by a Pharisee, an expert in religious law. Christ's response reveals a force higher than the law. Christ introduces a power which supersedes all laws - the law of love.

A woman who wears love is indescribably beautiful in the eyes of those she loves.

When my middle son Harry was six years old, we were watching The Voice Australia as a family. I was about to celebrate my fortieth birthday, and was on the hunt for the perfect birthday outfit.

So, each show, my main focus was on what dress Delta Goodrem (an Australian superstar judge) was wearing. Delta is absolutely stunning, and her outfits were spectacular. But my gorgeous six-year-old boy looked across at me and said, 'Mum, you are more beautiful than Delta.' My weary mother's heart melted.

Now, we know that me, dressed in my PJs with pulled-back hair, no make-up, and end of the day mother exhaustion visible on my face, was not looking nearly as gorgeous as Delta. But to my six-year-old son, who is loved by me, and loves me, I was absolutely beautiful. Love transforms us and makes us of great beauty in the eyes of those who are loved.

Love is a beautiful gown to wear. We all want to wear it and be known as a loving person. But keeping on this garment in the age we live in, is far from easy.

Jesus prophesied that in the last days,

> 'Because of the increase of wickedness, the love of most will grow cold'
> Matthew 24:12

The Message Bible puts it this way:

> 'For many others, the overwhelming spread of evil will do them in – nothing left of their love but a mound of ashes'
> Matthew 24:12

This is a sad and terrifying thought. That there will be such evil upon the earth that the love of most will grow cold.

There is a force around us and within us attempting to strip off our garments of love.

Author Francis Frangipane writes these challenging words:

'Is your love growing and becoming softer, brighter, more daring and more visible? Or is it becoming more discriminating, more calculating, less vulnerable and less available?

This is a very important issue, for your Christianity is only as real as your love. A measurable decrease in your ability to love is evidence that a stronghold of cold love is developing within you.

...It is inevitable that, in a world of increasing harshness and cruelty, we will at some point be hurt. But if we fail to react with love and forgiveness, if we retain in our spirit the debt the offender owes, that offence will rob our hearts of their capacity to love.

Imperceptibly, we will become a member of the majority of end-time Christians whose love is growing cold.' [32]

Life will attempt to rip off our garment of love.

If you have been alive long enough, it is highly likely you have been mistreated and hurt at some point. For some of us, it is very deep hurt.

Perhaps you have been physically, sexually or emotionally abused. Maybe you have experienced painful betrayal or rejection or been exposed to violence. For others, there is relational pain at not such an extreme level, but nonetheless very hurtful.

When we have been hurt, the temptation in the face of pain and conflict is to wear garments of hatred, anger, self-protection, indifference and shrinking back.

There was a season in my life as a pastor, where I faced stinging false accusations and betrayal from several people who were close to me. It hurt like nothing I have ever experienced.

To be misunderstood, lied about and mistreated by the people you have loved and served is extremely painful.

It was a battle to continue to wear the garment of love.

The winds of adversity threatened this beautiful coverall garment. I was tempted to wear bitterness, hardness, cynicism and fear.

To not trust again, not love again, not lead again.

It took some time to piece together the wardrobe of my heart.

I had to choose to continue loving when I didn't want to love.

To choose to forgive and bless, when the natural me wanted to do the opposite.

And I had to ensure the hurt I experienced at the hands of some, was not carried over into other relationships.

Choosing to wear love when you have been hurt is one of the most Christ-like things you and I can do.

Our human love may have limits, but at any time we can access the unfailing and unconditional love found in Christ. It is a supernatural garment that has the capacity to love when our human love has run out.

It is human to feel intense feelings such as hatred, anger and fear. It is supernatural to choose to cast them off and wear your Jesus wardrobe.

In the words of Lisa Bevere, 'Acting human isn't large enough to steward what is inside of us.' [33]

We need our supergirl wardrobe for a supernatural path.

Continually choosing to put on the garment of love amid challenge, breaks the power of bitterness and fear over our lives, and positions us to live a life of power.

I love the words of poet and memoirist Maya Angelou:

> 'A wise woman wishes to be no-one's enemy: a wise woman refuses to be anyone's victim.'[34]

The following words are an expression of what God has taught me about love.

LAYERS OF LOVE

Woven wonder in the secret place,
Layers of love, waves of grace.
Formed and framed with a scarlet cord,
From the womb, loved and adored.

Made to wear a garment of love,
A reflection of what is found above.
To love and be loved, the most beautiful crown,
Layers of love, the ultimate gown.

But love is born on a battleground,
Where conflict and strife tear at our gown.
Our love can grow cold, and our sight grow dim,
Hatred and fear threaten to win.

But this garment awaits a woman strong,
A woman who discerns right from wrong.
A woman who forgives and lets go of pain,
A woman who yields to a different reign.

A reign of love and a reign of grace,
A rain that cleanses and covers mistakes.
For the layers of this gown heal the pain,
The weave of love breaks the chain.

Love's many layers transform our surrounds,
And guard our heart when darkness abounds.
So, slip off hatred, rejection and fear,
Put on this garment that is always near.

Know you are loved and wear it bold,
This garment that will never grow old.
Love others well, and the game will change,
For when all else fails, love remains.

CLOTHED IN POWER

'I am going to send you what my Father has promised; but stay in the city until you have been clothed with power from on high.'
Luke 24:49

When Jesus left the earth, He told His disciples to wait in Jerusalem until they were clothed with power from on high.

Jesus was referring to the coming of the Holy Spirit.

There is a supernatural power from God available that will cause us to achieve and accomplish things that we could never do in our own strength.

The disciples were commissioned with a mighty mission.

To preach the gospel; the stunning forgiveness of sins and promise of eternal life to all nations. But they were never asked to do it without The provision of a power suit that came straight from the heavens.

There have been many seasons in my life where I have forgotten the power suit that is available to me in Christ.

As a young, exhausted mum, overwhelmed with the demands of motherhood and ministry, there have been times when my bed was my best friend, and the effort to rise was enormous.

In one of these seasons, my youngest child Elijah, who was four at the time, jumped into bed with me, cupped my head in his hands and looked straight into my eyes. 'Mum, don't forget you have superpowers.' And I knew those words were straight from the heart of God.

We so easily forget we have superpowers and we faint under the atmospheric pressures of this world.

In effect, Christ said to the disciples: 'You have a power suit from heaven, that is needed for everything I have called you to. Don't consider leaving home without it.'

Some of us are filled with passion and vision to live a magnificent life that brings glory to God, but we need our power suit.

Be encouraged by this poem etched below for daughters of the earth. Daughters called to supernatural missions.

Don't forget your power suit.

CLOTHED IN POWER

Heavenly visions flood her head,
A life with purpose; meaningless shed.
To walk on paths etched in time,
To live out purpose, alive in the climb.

Set apart for a noble cause,
To make a difference in the midst of wars.
To bring great good upon the earth,
This purpose ordained before her birth.

Yet, natural garments drag her down,
Human abilities limit her crown.
Her resources wane at the task at hand,
Her own strength drains like the sand.

She needs a garment from another place,
Beyond herself, electricity laced.
And as she waits come winds of grace,
That lift her higher to finish her race.

Now clothed in power, not of this world,
Heaven's energy, purpose unfurled.
When her spirit faints, she claims this gown,
Now clothed in power, she wears her crown.

CROWNED IN BEAUTY

'...bestow on them a crown of beauty, instead of ashes...'
Isaiah 61:3

As I found myself in the final stages of writing the manuscript for this book, I debated whether to include the crown of beauty that the Lord bestows in the place of ashes.

It is not one of the heavenly garments that I regularly teach on. But something about this crown has captured my heart.

When sin entered the Garden of Eden, paradise was lost. What was once idyllic and beautiful became polluted by death, destruction, violence and toil. Beauty to ashes.

The promise of Isaiah 61 is the restoration of beauty. The restoration of what was lost.

> *For as the soil makes the sprout come up and a garden causes seeds to grow, so the sovereign Lord will make righteousness and praise spring up before all nations.*
> *Isaiah 61:11 NIV*

I love that the imagery of this passage is the imagery of the garden. There is a yearning in the heart of God to bring His sons and daughters back to the beauty of the garden, back to all things good, noble, pure and lovely.

Amid a world torn and polluted by war, violence and sin, God calls His people to continually choose to behold beauty, to see what is good.

I believe that this crown of beauty speaks of our thought life.

Returning our thought life back to the garden, back to all things good and beautiful.

It was from a prison cell, that Paul encouraged us to fix our thoughts on all that is good.

> Finally, brothers and sisters, whatever is true, whatever is noble, whatever is right, whatever is pure, whatever is lovely, whatever is admirable – if anything is excellent or praiseworthy – think about such things.
> Philippians 4:8

If Paul can fix his thoughts while he was in a prison cell, we can certainly fix our thoughts on all things good and lovely amid the challenges of our own life.

It is a call to be crowned with beauty amid the craziness of life — to behold beauty, to fix our thoughts on what is good and lovely.

It may mean letting go of the ashes, the disappointments, the griefs, the losses, but the price is worth it. A crown of beauty bestowed by the Lord.

It is time to straighten our crown ladies, to fix our thoughts on all that is true, noble, pure, lovely, admirable, excellent and praiseworthy. Time to let go of the ashes to wear His beauty.

His kingdom on earth, as it is in heaven.

Part Five

DRESSED FOR DESTINY

Chapter Thirty-Six

SHAKE OFF THE DUST

'Shake off your dust'
Isaiah 52:2

Now that we are dressed, it is time to shake off the dust.

Life has a way of coating us with dust.

We may be all dressed up in our new creation identity in Christ. Then we walk through the city streets, or a chaotic day at home, or desert terrain, or a gritty mission field, and we find our beautiful garments coated in dust. We don't feel so shiny anymore.

The grime of daily life gets in our air passages, and we labour to breathe.

Dust covers our clothes, and their glory is dimmed.

The grit gets in our eyes, and it is hard to see.

Vision becomes blurred.

The dust coats our mouth, and the pure water of our words become dirty.

The Prophet was clear: shake off your dust.

This needs to become a daily discipline.

To shake off the dust of everyday life, the dust of desert lands and disappointments. To shake off the dust of yesterday so we can live bright and shiny today.

Each day is new.

Each day we rise and dress.

Each day we shake off the dust we've gathered along the way.

When Jesus sent His disciples out, He was clear.

> *And if anyone doesn't listen to you and rejects your message, when you leave that house or town, shake the dust off your feet as a prophetic act that you will not take their defilement with you.* Matthew 10:14 TPT

Some of us need to shake off rejection.

We may need to shake off the disappointment of an appointment that didn't work out.

We all need to shake off the dust of past assignments to adequately fulfil the opportunities that God has for each of us.

The Hebrew word for shake is *na'ar* which literally means shaking out of a lion's mane.

Can you imagine a lion pinned to the ground by a little dust? No, the lion would rise with a roar, shake off the dust from his glorious mane and pace towards his prey.

You and I are called to have this same response.

To declare *na'ar* to the enemy. To rise, shake off the dust and move towards the next assignment God has for us.

Chapter Thirty-Seven

SIT ENTHRONED

'Sit enthroned, Jerusalem!'
Isaiah 52:2 TPT

The best way to stay dressed in the royal garments Christ has provided for you is to remember your throne and sit in it often.

'And God raised us up with Christ and seated us with Him in the heavenly realms in Christ Jesus,'
Ephesians 2:6 NIV

When we receive Christ as our Lord and Saviour, we change our address. We are most at home in the heavenly places, in the realm of God's presence, sitting on our royal throne as daughters of God. But we have a tendency to forget our identity and become entangled in the affairs of the world.

As daughters of a King, we need to regularly dwell in the secret place of His presence, remembering we have free access. It is our rightful address and a place to sit above the battles of the world.

It is from this place that we meet with God and pray. It is the secret place of strength—a place I depend on and visit often.

I pray, not because I have to, but because I need to.

I need to talk to God. I need to hear from my heavenly Father and experience His presence every day.

I need to make my requests before the King, and I need to yield to His perspective on my world and the challenges that I face. His view is always through a lens of faith, hope and love. When I find myself outside the zone of faith, hope and love, it is a sure sign that it is time to visit the throne room.

Even this morning, I woke with grey clouds enshrouding my mind, unable to see a way through particular challenges. I rang trusted friends who had no answers and left me more frustrated.

I knew I had to visit the throne room.

Godly counsel is integral to our journey, but it is no substitute for the throne room. It will never replace our personal audience with the King. He is a jealous and loving King, and eager to be our, *'Wonderful Counsellor'*, our *'Mighty God'*, our *'Everlasting Father'* and our *'Prince of Peace'* (Isaiah 9:6).

This morning as I entered His presence, in answer to my plight, I heard the following words: 'When you don't know which way to go, I AM the way to go.'

So often we want clear direction, and fail to see that God is the direction and that Jesus is the way. That impossibilities in the natural demand we go deeper in the supernatural. Deeper in prayer. Lack of answers in the courts of earth send us to the courts of heaven, where we find the mercy, wisdom, strength and the kindness of a heavenly King.

As beautifully expressed in Hebrews 4:16:

> *'Let us then approach God's throne of grace with confidence, so that we may receive mercy and find grace to help us in our time of need.'*

Psalm 45 speaks of the wonder of the royal bride, called out of one kingdom and into another. Drawn by the passion of the King into His royal chamber.

> *Listen, daughter, and pay careful attention:*
> *Forget your people and your father's house.*
> *Let the King be enthralled by your beauty:*
> *Honor him, for he is your Lord…*
> *All glorious is the princess within her chamber;*
> *Her gown is interwoven with gold.*
> *In embroidered garments she is led to the King;*
> *Psalm 45:10-11,13-1*

The adornment of this princess and the priceless value of her gown is woven in the secret place of the palace of the King.

I will never forget my visit to the City Palace in Jaipur, India. A tapestry of artistry and colour in the midst of a stunning city. Lost in the beauty of the palace, I wandered through its many rooms, decorated doorways, and royal courts.

We had paid for the private tour of royal rooms only recently opened to the public and were led through secret passageways to the upper rooms. We stopped on the top floor and entered what felt like a secret chamber of beauty, a highly decorated room of mirrors and jewels knowns as the Hall of Beauty. I sat on its cushioned floor, sinking deep into imaginations of the life of a princess in her royal chamber. As we stepped out of this room, on the right was a similar room known as the Dressing Room of the Princess.

This room was converted to a small store selling replicas from the royal wardrobe. I stepped into the change room and dressed in one of the replicas from the wardrobe of the princess. Of course, the girls with me encouraged me to buy the dress, and I travelled home with a garment purchased in the dressing room of the princess.

This dress, though beautiful, will one day fade, but the beauty that comes from being dressed in the secret place of the King is unfading. The garments purchased by faith in the presence of the King are woven with gold, representing holiness, a life set-apart and a beauty that never fades.

The royal daughter is dressed in the secret place of the King's palace, and we continually return, remembering our throne and our royal address.

THERE IS A ROOM WHERE DAUGHTERS DWELL

There is a room where daughters dwell,
A place of power where lies dispel,
A place of thrones, tall and grand,
Where heavenly daughters take their stand.

A place that's ruled by the King of Kings,
Light and truth found within.
A place our Saviour sits enthroned,
Our weaknesses, failings, completely atoned.

A place to petition at the feet of the King,
Freedom, blue sky, a place to sing.
A place to frequent every day,
A heavenly realm, from where we pray.

Stepping through the doors of grace,
His sceptre extends with loving embrace.
And from His courts, we make our claim.
With authority declaring His eternal reign.

And every promise becomes our prose,
As we walk with victory upon our foes.
A place from where we take our ground,
And our life becomes heaven's sound.

Chapter Thirty-Eight

BACK TO THE GARDEN

And the Lord God planted a garden toward the east, in Eden [delight]; and there He put the man whom He had formed (framed, constituted).

And out of the ground the Lord God made to grow every tree that is pleasant to the sight or to be desired — good (suitable, pleasant) for food; the tree of life also in the center of the garden, and the tree of the knowledge of [the difference between] good and evil and blessing and calamity.

Now a river went out of Eden to water the garden; and from there it divided and became four [river] heads. The first is named Pishon; it is the one flowing around the whole land of Havilah, where there is gold.

The gold of that land is of high quality; bdellium and onyx stone are there. The second river is named Gihon; it is the one flowing around the whole land of Cush. The third river is named Hiddekel [the Tigris]; it is the one flowing east of Assyria. And the fourth river is the Euphrates.

And the Lord God took the man and put him in the Garden of Eden to tend and guard and keep it.
Genesis 2:8-15 AMPC

The journey of the first daughter began in a garden. A garden of beauty and fruitfulness. A garden of intimacy. A fertile playground for the sons and daughters of God.

You will notice that this garden is a place of delight. A place where the trees are pleasing to the eye and good for food. The Lord created a world where His children would be sustained with beauty and wonder, and also with the essential sustenance needed for the human body.

It is helpful to remember that we need both. We are created for beauty and wonder, just as we are made to need food.

You will also notice that four rivers are running through the garden. The first river is named Pishon, meaning 'increase'. The second, Gihon, meaning 'bursting forth'. The third, Hiddekel, meaning 'rapid', and the fourth, Euphrates, meaning 'fruitfulness'.

Imagine a garden where the waters running through it are waters of increase, waters that burst forth, rapid waters and waters that cause fruitfulness. These are the waters that I want irrigating the garden of my life.

One of the most devastating passages in scripture is given in the next chapter of Genesis.

> And the Lord God said, Behold, the man has become like one of Us [the Father, Son, and Holy Spirit], to know [how to distinguish between] good and evil and blessing and calamity; and now, lest he put forth his hand and take also from the tree of life and eat, and live forever—Therefore the Lord God sent him forth from the Garden of Eden to till the ground from which he was taken. So [God] drove out the man; and He placed at the east of the Garden of Eden the cherubim and a flaming sword which turned every way, to keep and guard the way to the tree of life. Genesis 3:22-24 AMPC

Ever since humanity was sent forth from the garden, there has been a cry in us to return. To return to the place where the Lord walks with us in the cool of the day.

The place where rivers of increase, abundance and life run free - a place of beauty and fruitfulness entwined as one.

It was the cry of the human heart and the passion of the Father that brought Christ to the earth and ultimately sent him to another garden, the garden of Gethsemane.

> Then Jesus went with them to a garden called Gethsemane and told his disciples, "Stay here while I go over there and pray." Taking along Peter and the two sons of Zebedee, he plunged into an agonizing sorrow. Then he said, "This sorrow is crushing my life

out. Stay here and keep vigil with me." Going a little ahead, he fell on his face, praying, "My Father, if there is any way, get me out of this. But please, not what I want. You, what do you want?" Matthew 26:36-39 MSG

In the garden of Gethsemane, Christ began a journey that would give humankind the key to go back to the garden. The Cross is our key back to the garden; our key to returning to a place of beauty, blessing, intimacy and peace.

As I write this chapter, we are still in the COVID-19 crisis. As a pastor, this is a challenging time as there is currently no blue sky for unrestricted gatherings of people. It is challenging to plan, not yet being able to see a clear path ahead.

Yet in this season of restriction, there is unrestricted access to the garden of intimacy with the Lord. And I hear the undeniable call of God beckoning us back to the garden. A place to rest, a place to refresh, a place to be loved, a place to be sustained, a place to behold beauty, a place to hear His voice.

We spend so much time in the dry, dusty and thorny lands of earth and forget to inhabit the beautiful and fruitful garden of intimacy available to us in Christ. We do well to remember that we are 'in the world, but not of the world'[35]. The home of our spirit is another place we need to frequent for regular refreshment.

Our spirit can be stained and deflated by the ugliness of what we see around us. Still, in a moment, it can be cleansed and inflated by the fresh air of the garden of the Lord.

Time in the garden helps us to wear our spiritual wardrobe with beauty and wonder. It is from the garden of intimacy with Him that Jesus creates beautiful, unique and fruitful gardens within us.

This is beautifully articulated in Song of Songs.

> *Your inward life is now sprouting,*
> *Bringing forth fruit.*
> *What a beautiful paradise unfolds within you.*
> *When I'm near you I smell aromas of the finest spice*
> *For many clusters of my exquisite fruit now grow within*

your inner garden.
Here are nine:
Pomegranates of passion,
Henna from heaven,
Spikenard so sweet,
Saffron shining,
Fragrant calamus from the Cross,
Sacred cinnamon,
Branches of scented woods,
Myrrh, like tears from a tree,
And aloe as eagles ascending.
Your life flows into mine, pure as a garden spring.
A well of living water springs up from within you,
Like a mountain brook flowing into my heart!
Song of Songs 4:13-15 TPT

The fruits and spices in this verse represent many aspects of the work of the Cross in our life. The pomegranate represents worship and the exultation of Christ. Henna comes from a word meaning ransom price. Spikenard represents light. Saffron is a lover's perfume. Calamus comes from a word meaning redeemed. Cinnamon is the aroma of holiness. Myrrh is a spice formed from cutting a tree, representing Christ's suffering, and aloe is a healing balm.[36]

It is the work of the heavenly gardener to cause the flourishing garden of our inner life to speak and breathe the work of the Cross and the wonder of Christ. Time in the garden with the Lord changes the garden of our heart, so our fragrance is sweet and brings heaven to earth.

When we are diligent to journey back to the garden, it always has an overflow.

My Beloved, one with me in my garden,
How marvellous
That my friends, the brides-to-be,
Now hear your voice and song.
Song of Songs 8:13 TPT

For we are fellow workmen (joint promoters, laborers together) with and for God; you are God's [a]garden and vineyard and field under cultivation, [you are] God's building.
1 Corinthians 3:9 AMP

Every day we live in the duality of beauty and battle.

Taking time in the garden of the Lord; in a place of intimacy and wonder with Him, equips us to bring heaven to a desperate and hungry earth.

Chapter Thirty-Nine

DAUGHTERS IN TRAINING

A few years ago, I was asked to share The Invisible She message with a gathering of experienced and successful pastors, both men and women. My initial reaction was hesitation.

My thinking was that this was an elementary teaching for women; a foundational doctrine for new believers.

Nonetheless, I sat down to prepare, and the Holy Spirit came alongside to breathe new layers into this message. Layers of truth for all believers, revelation of the processes of God for His sons and daughters.

So long as we live in the human body, we will find ourself regularly needing to update our spiritual wardrobe. A garment of joy that was a comfortable fit in a season of blessing needs to be updated during seasons of trial to become a deeper joy, a joy worn through challenges. Or a garment of strength that fitted well before children were born collapses under the strain of children and household management. It needs to be updated to a greater level of strength.

The challenges of life have a way of bringing awareness to the limits of our humanity. This is designed to lead us back to the Cross, to once again engage in the great exchange. Our humanity for His divinity. Our brokenness for His wholeness. Our weakness for His strength. There is no shame in having to regularly update our spiritual wardrobe. The wardrobe at the foot of the Cross is designed for daily visits, sometimes even hourly.

Hebrews 12 is an incredible chapter on the race we run as believers. It speaks of the great cloud of witnesses that cheer us on as we run with endurance the race that is set before us. It encourages us to look to Jesus, and the example He set as He fixed His eyes on the prize before Him.

From verse five, the chapter speaks of the often avoided, but very real topic of the Lord's training of His sons and daughters as they run their race.

Interestingly, the Greek word for training in this passage is the word *gumnazo* (where we get the word gymnasium), and the word means to strip down, exercise naked, to train.[37]

Progressing in our journey with God is like voluntarily signing up to a spiritual gymnasium.

A gym where we strip off, and regularly the true state of our nakedness is exposed. A place we become aware over and over again of our need for new clothes.

Like the gym, we can see this as a blessing or a curse. But it is God's heart that this training is a blessing.

> *'Fully embrace God's correction as part of your training for he is doing what any loving father does for his children. For who has ever heard of a child who never had to be corrected? We all should welcome God's discipline as the validation of authentic sonship. For if we have never once endured his correction it only proves we are strangers and not sons.'*
> Hebrews 12:7-8 TPT

The awareness of our naked form continually drives us to our Saviour.

And regular wardrobe updates increase our spiritual beauty.

Chapter Forty
PATHS OF PURPOSE

> For 'we have become His poetry, a re-created people that will fulfil the destiny he has given each of us, for we are joined to Jesus, the Anointed One. Even before we were born, God planned in advance our destiny and the good works we would do to fulfil it.'
> Ephesians 2:10 TPT

Great appointments await a woman dressed well. A woman dressed for success. Who knows, you just might find yourself going for a spacewalk, or a supernatural mission across the globe, or perhaps working the wonders of heaven in the midst of your very own home.

It is time for God's daughters to understand and dress in the fullness of our heavenly identity, in order to take up heaven's many assignments for the daughters of God.

There are places and missions etched out in the plans of heaven for the woman dressed in the knowledge of who she is in Christ.

The birthing of this book has come as I have dressed in my own heavenly wardrobe. Choosing by faith to believe that I am who He says I am. Any ministry I have engaged in that has borne heavenly fruit has come from a place of being clothed in the garments of my heavenly identity. And even the love I spread in my own home grows as I learn to dress myself in Christ.

Now, it's your turn. Let the spirit of God whisper to your heart and dress you with wonder, love, beauty and grace for His kingdom purpose. And may His will be done in and through your life, on earth as it is in heaven.

I'll see you out there on God's beautiful paths of purpose.

Love,

Kirrily xx

PATHS OF PURPOSE

Ancient paths engraved in time,
Etched with purpose, hands divine.
The artistry of heaven upon the earth,
Plans ordained from her birth.

But she laid captive, blind to this land,
Where her life is a poem, redemption planned.
So, wake now daughter, shake off the dust.
Dress in your beauty, step out with trust.

For every dawn writes your name.
Calling you out on paths to claim.
Through open doors and passages wild.
Custom created, uniquely styled.

Paths that wind through sun and rain.
A tapestry of purpose, singing your name.

Breathe faith in a master plan,
Walk on paths not made by man.
Own your story and don't look down.
Your footsteps are life to the world around.

ENDNOTES

Chapter 1: Naked But Clothed
1 Ann Voskamp, *The Broken Way* (Zondervan, USA, 2016) p7

Chapter 3: Who Dressed You Today?
2 https://edition.cnn.com/2019/03/25/us/nasa-first-all-female-spacewalk-canceled-trnd/index.html
3 Steven Furtick (@stevenfurtick) Instagram Photo

Chapter 5: Ripping Off Rejection
4 John 8:44
5 Luke 22:42
6 Matthew 27:46, Mark 15:34
7 Mark 3:21
8 Hebrews 13:12

Chapter 7: Dressed in Disappointment
9 Matthew 11:29
10 Joyce Meyer, *Why, God, Why?* (Warner Books, 1995, New York)

Chapter 12: Fig Leaves of All Kinds
11 Tim Keller, *The Meaning of Marriage: Facing the Complexities of Commitment with the Wisdom of God*, (Hodder & Stoughton, London, 2011)

Chapter 18: Awake, Awake
12 Katherine Ruonala, *From Wilderness to Wonder*, (Charisma House, Florida, 2015) Chapter 5
13 2 Corinthians 1:3-4

Chapter 20: Dressed in Salvation
14 C S Lewis, *The Lion, the Witch and the Wardrobe: The Chronicles of Narnia* (Geoffrey Bles, 1950, UK) Aslan is the name of the lion in this book. Aslan is widely recognised as a literary representation of Christ in this series.

Chapter 22: Clothed in Strength
15 Audrey Hepburn as quoted in BrainyQuote, https://www.brainyquote.com/quotes/audrey_hepburn_413480
16 Joel 3:10
17 2 Corinthians 12:7-10
18 Oprah Winfrey *What I Know For Sure* (MacMillan, 2015, London)

Chapter 23: Dressed in Dignity
19 YourDictionary.com, Love To Know, 2020, https://www.yourdictionary.com/dignity

Chapter 26: The Garment of Praise
20 "Spark joy" is phrase introduced and used by Marie Kondo in the Netflix Series Tidying Up with Marie Kondo 2019
21 Corrie Ten Boom, *The Hiding Place* (Chosen Books, 1971, Netherlands)

Chapter 28: Clothed in Compassion
22 Dictionary.com, Dictionary.com 2021, https://www.dictionary.com/browse/compassion
23 Paul Glynn, *The Wayside Stream: Reconciliation*, (Marist Fathers Books, 2003, Australia) pp 12-20

Chapter 29: Clothed in Kindness
24 Kirrily Lowe, *Kindness, The Invisible Tree*, (Wombat Books, 2016, QLD)
25 Kirrily Lowe, *Kindness, The Invisible Tree*

Chapter 30: The Garment of Humility
26 Matthew 4:3-6
27 Luke 23:37-39

Chapter 31: Graced with Gentleness
28 Erwin McManus, *The Way of the Warrior*, (Waterbrook, 2019, USA) Introduction
29 Erwin McManus, *The Way of the Warrior*, Introduction

Chapter 32: Clothed in Patience
30 The Cambridge Dictionary, Cambridge University Press, 2021, https://dictionary.cambridge.org/dictionary/english/patience
31 Kirrily Lowe, *Patience, The Invisible Tree*, (Wombat Books, 2013, QLD)

Chapter 33: Layers of Love
32 Frances Frangipane, *The Three Battlegrounds*, (Arrow Publications, 2006, USA) p67,68)
33 Lisa Bevere as quoted on Instagram @lisabevere
34 Maya Angelou as quoted on BrainyQuote https://www.brainyquote.com/quotes/maya_angelou_578805

Chapter 38: Back to the Garden
35 John 17:14-16
36 Song of Songs 4:13-14 TPT (see TPT footnotes of these verses)

Chapter 39: Daughters in Training
37 Tim Keller, *Walking with God Through Pain & Suffering*, (Hodder & Stougton, 2015, London) p193

ACKNOWLEDGEMENTS

This message, this book and this project has been a labour of love over almost a decade. Many people have woven in and out of this stunning vision to bring to life the Christ-given identity of a woman through words, poetry, fashion, music and design. So, here we go...

Thanks to the incredible **fashion designers** who God knitted to the heart of this project to bring to life the garments of a woman's identity.

Anjna Seth is the designer of the Garments of Strength, Dignity, Love, Courage, Peace and Power. Anjna, you were an unexpected and stunning gift, a dream to work with, and the perfect designer to launch this project in your beautiful nation, India. I am thankful you caught the heart of this project, and it has impacted your life as much as the Garments you have designed have impacted many.

Tarese Epere is the designer of the Garments of Joy, Praise, Gentleness and Compassion. Tarese, I was told you were destined for this project from the start. Your gift of delicate, bold, intricate and statement design is straight from heaven. The beauty God has created through your own brokenness is the heart of this project, and I am so glad I finally got the courage to make contact with you and that you said YES.

The Invisible She uses the language of fashion to present the gospel. The true beauty, however, is always in the **women modelling** the dresses. Thank you to the stunning women who have volunteered their time to model the Garments shown in this book. Some have graced the garments on catwalks, and some have been photographed for this book.

Thank you **Nat Marquardt**, for modelling Salvation, Love and Dignity so well. **Grace Rowe** for wearing Kindness and Peace with beauty and grace. **Grace Kim** for a stunning portrayal of Patience, Truth and Gentleness. Anointed songstress **Erin McKeller** in the Garment of Praise. Beautiful **Sarah Samuels** crowned with Beauty. Stunning

Nicole Madell, the original model for the Garment of Strength. **Lisa Bocarro** for bravely and beautifully modelling Love. **Gabby de Gersigny**, our beautiful Eve, and the model for Compassion, Peace, Dignity, Humility and Power.

Ladies, you are all unique, beautiful and anointed from the inside out. Thank you for gracing these pages and believing in this message.

In 2016 **Gary Compton** travelled with myself and a team to India, where the Garments of Strength and Dignity were created and presented for the first time. Since that time, Gary has volunteered his time and talent to photograph the Invisible She Garments. Gary, thank you for capturing the images that feature in this book – they are stunning! Thank you also to **Pete Sutherland** and **Ang Mundumbwila** for their assistance on The Invisible She photoshoot.

Chloe Hubbard, you caught the vision for The Invisible She Project 7 years ago and have always been all in. I am thankful for the passion and beauty you brought to these images through hair and makeup. Thank you, **Jen Eadie**, who came alongside Chloe to bring these images to life with your heart for God and gift of hair and makeup. And beautiful **Claire Marrinan** in India always cheering on The Invisible She and bringing your talent to this project in the face of Strength.

A deep and heartfelt thank you to my beautiful and passionate pastor friend **Rachel Waters**, who took a gamble and said yes to launching this project with the women of Selah Church, Mumbai, India. The beauty and richness of your nation has been the perfect seedbed for the beauty and life this message carries. Thank you for holding hands with me and showcasing this project's first six Garments over four consecutive years. Thank you to the women of Selah Church who caught this message, modelled the Garments, hosted events, and many times spoke of the book to come.

An enormous thank you is owed to my activator friend **Amanda Viviers**, whose activation gift propelled me to finally complete this manuscript. Thank you for believing in this project and my writing and helping me take tangible steps to bring this book baby to life.

As COVID-19 hit Sydney in 2020, an unexpected gift arrived for this project. This gift has literally touched every page of this manuscript and even sneakily modelled some Garments. The beautiful, deep, prophetic and creative **Taylor-Kate Brosnahan** is the graphic designer behind the images and pages of this book and has woven beauty and life throughout. You will find her modelling Joy and Righteousness. I am grateful for her carrying this message in her heart and helping birth it with creativity and beauty.

This manuscript has passed through the hands of many before it has seen the light of the day. Beautiful **Sarah Chan**, you were the first to read this manuscript and bring your suggestions from a young woman's perspective. Thank you for your constant encouragement in the releasing of this message.

Em Hazledean, thank you for being my first professional editor. Thanks for catching this message from the start, encouraging me to share more of my story and seeking to draw out the gold. Thank you, **Pam Borrow**, for a theological edit that I passed – yay! Thank you to my friend **Ruth Browning** for reading the manuscript and your guidance and wisdom throughout. Thank you, **Nola Passmore** and **Ellena Tankard** for your thorough edit. And beautiful **Jessie Cox** for reading through with diligence and care.

Thanks to the Hutch Touch - **Clint** and **Andrea Hutchison**, who arrived for this project's final stages, to help birth this book with beauty and elegance. Thank you!

Thanks to the pastors and leaders who have released this message in their own church and encouraged me throughout this project's duration.

Thank you, **Ps Cathie Green**, **Ps Mike** and **Joy Connell**, **Ps David** and **Kate Connell**, **Ps Claude** and **Carolyn Carrello**, **Ps Marty** and **Elly Webb** and **Ps Phil** and **Julie Oldfield**. Thanks to my friends in ministry, **Ps Isi de Gersigny**, **Ps Richard** and **Sue Botta**, **Vicki Simpson**, **Ps Andrew** and **Janine Kubala**, **Ps Vanessa Hoyes**, **Heidi Wysman** and **Ps Katherine Ruonala**, for your encouragement with this message and for your endorsements in this book.

Thanks also to my friends **Cath Foote**, **Deb McIntyre** and **John** and **Monica Ford** for your encouragement, and to **Henry** and **Genevieve Clay-Smith**, for catching the heart and vision in the early days. And beautiful **Lady Tre (Tre Boyd)** for bringing fresh and fun sound to this project. Thanks to **Dietrich Marquardt** for helping with legalities along the way.

Thanks to the founding pastors of our C3 Church movement, **Ps Phil and Chris Pringle**, who began a move of God with creativity and colour at its core. The creativity in my ministry was birthed in this atmosphere, and I am so grateful for your love and encouragement throughout my journey.

Thanks to our beautiful church, **God In The City**, that has not only pulled this message out of my heart as I have sought to minister to the women of our city but has been a seedbed of creativity and life for bringing heaven to earth.

Thanks to the **women** who have opened their hearts to this message and sent me their stories of transformation. It is the daughters of God who are at the heart of the purpose of this book.

Thanks to **my mum** and **my family**, who think anything I write is magnificent!

Thanks to my gorgeous boys **Sam, Harry**, and **Elijah**, who are the adorable chiselling instruments that the Lord has used to make me the woman I am and think it is cool that Mum writes books.

Thanks to **my husband, Tim**, who believed in this vision from the start, loves my poetry, cheers me on, and is 100% committed to bringing to life with me a larger than life dream.

And the greatest acknowledgement goes to the lover of my soul, **Jesus Christ**, who birthed this wild, beautiful and all-consuming dream in my heart, and is the true Author and Finisher of my salvation and transformation as a woman.

So thankful.

Kirrily xx

ABOUT THE AUTHOR

Kirrily Lowe is a pastor and author from the Northern Beaches of Sydney, Australia. Since 2002, Kirrily has been a Senior Minister alongside her husband Tim of God In The City, a C3 congregation in the inner-city of Sydney.

Kirrily is passionate about seeing women released into their God-given identity and is known for communicating this through creative, poetic and colourful mediums, using teaching, poetry and fashion to bring full expression to this message.

Kirrily is also the author of The Invisible Tree series; a delightful and fun series of Children's books. Kirrily began her career as a lawyer before sensing a call into pastoral ministry.

Pastor Tim and Kirrily live in Sydney with their three boys, Samuel, Harrison and Elijah. Her life is full as a wife, mum, minister, learner and writer.

You can find out more about Kirrily, or make contact with her at www.kirrilylowe.com

OTHER BOOKS BY KIRRILY LOWE

The Invisible Tree series:
(Children's Picture Books)

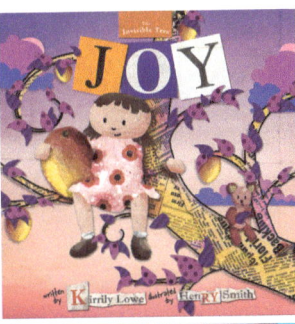

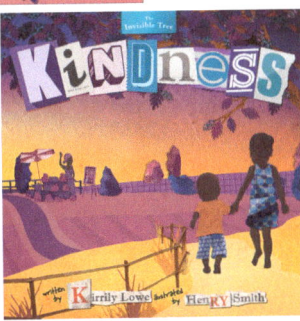

The Invisible Tree series is also available at

kirrilylowe.com
or
theinvisibletree.com.au

www.ingramcontent.com/pod-product-compliance
Lightning Source LLC
Chambersburg PA
CBHW042049290426
44110CB00001B/3